Activate Your Power

and
Launch Your
DREAM Business

Noelle Marie Amendola
10/20/2015

Contents

Introduction

Are You Ready to Actualize Your Power and Greatness?

If you were drawn to this book, I'm guessing you already know that you have insane potential within you.

You've always felt it.

You know you're pretty awesome.

You've done the inner work.

You are in touch with your dreams and visions.

You know that you have what it takes to inspire, awaken, encourage, and heal the world.

You know your destiny is important.

You may have already written a book or created a product or you have a service ready to offer people.

And you know the world needs it.

You know the world needs YOU and everything you have to give.

But something is blocking you from fully releasing and giving and sharing everything you have with the world. Something is blocking you from actually *connecting* with all those people who need you. Something is blocking you from fully SHINING and SHARING everything you have created.

You know it's time.

And you even know how to embrace and walk with your fears. It's not just about fear, and you know it.

You are DYING to rise to that level of greatness and success you see in your dreams and in those you admire, but HOW?

How do you actually activate your power and turn these creative passions into a lucrative, thriving, mission-driven business that will change the world?

THAT is why I've written this book and created the concurrent course in the School for Dreamers.

There is an answer.

There is a glorious answer!

And it's not about striving or pushing, or creating a plan.

It's not about copying what your hero is doing.

It's not about willpower or just "putting in the work."

It's about a new outrageous level of embracing your Highest Self,

a new level of focus,

a new level of fiercely strong boundaries.

It's about finally creating the SPACE for you to do ONLY what you love.

It's about letting go of all those outdated, limiting thoughts you have about MONEY,

and fully welcoming the abundance that is waiting to flood your life.

It's about empowering yourself to ASK for what you want.

To RECEIVE what you've asked for.

And then to be able to CELEBRATE when you've arrived at that new level of abundance and power.

And most of all, it's about giving yourself crazy, unbounded, outrageous permission to SHINE,

to be your own hero,

to do this dream business in the exact, unique, powerful way that is EASY for you.

Yes, that's right – there is a magical WAY for you to do this thing.

A unique way designed JUST for you, that will feel EASY, LIGHT, JOYFUL, and effortless.

The key to this unique path is inside you.

The POWER inside you is unlimited.

But this power is lying dormant, crying out to you.

It's waiting for you to learn how to release it, to activate it, to fully let it out so it can transform the world around you.

There is no time to wait.

There is a hurting, sleeping world that needs everything you came here to give.

The time is NOW.

Let's DO this!

How This Book Joyfully Emerged

I did not plan to write this book.

I did not *expect* to write this book.

I have a list of 10 books I want to write, and this one was not anywhere on that list.

In fact, the book I *thought* would be my second book, *Life Beyond Fear*, was already started and well on its way when Life took me on another path which led me here.

Activate Your Power and Launch Your DREAM Business is a very special book that has a magical life of its own, which is a part of me but also completely *beyond* me.

I actually started writing this book before I even knew it WAS a book.

And then once I knew what was happening and received clarity about the title and the full chapter outline, it flowed out of me in a few days.

I was in the ZONE as I wrote it.

Completely overwhelmed by joy and passion, I sat down every day at various coffee shops in Marquette, Michigan and literally laughed out loud in ecstasy and amazement as the words flowed through me into my computer.

I am learning everything in this book right along with you.

This is where I am in my journey, right now.

I felt this book being written *through* me, not from me. The process was magical and effortless, and I am sitting here in complete AWE at what happens when we just trust in Spirit to guide us. Magical books get written through us, like this one, when we just allow ourselves to ENJOY what we love doing.

I love to journal, and this book started in my journal. I was feeling a sense of a *pulling away* of my new self from my old self. I was feeling the desire to step more fully into my power, to fully embrace the leadership role I'm destined to have on the earth.

One morning a few weeks ago in Boulder, Colorado I was sitting by myself journaling with my cup of coffee, up in a mountain-top home in which Vince and I were staying for a week.

I was in my most happy place, alone with my journal, free to connect with the deepest part of ME.

Pure heaven.

Very spontaneously and with no thought whatsoever of writing a book, I started writing out little statements which defined what a Powerful Person was.

How do Powerful People act? How do Powerful People think?

Statements like,

> ## Powerful People LOVE to SHINE.

And all of a sudden, I had 42 statements about Powerful People.

I loved these little powerful quotes.

These quotes inspired me.

And immediately I thought, *I wonder what these are for? People need to read these!*

And as I started dividing them into categories, I noticed 6 *themes* emerge, which became the chapter titles of this book.

1 - The Power of VISION

2 - The Power WITHIN

3 - The Power of FOCUS

4 - The Power of ABUNDANCE

5 - The Power of BOLDNESS

6 - The Power of UNIQUENESS

You can read all of these quotes at the back of this book, in the addendum, but I also scattered them throughout the book in various places. Make sure to read the addendum in order to enjoy all of them, because not all of them made it into the chapters themselves. They're all precious to me and inspiring statements of how we can step fully into our POWER!

These spiritual nuggets of pure treasure were the beginning and the foundation for this powerful book.

Along with this book, I have also created a concurrent online course in the School for Dreamers. If you wish to dig much deeper into this topic, to have group support and coaching, and watch inspiring weekly video lessons with thought-provoking writing assignments, then I encourage you to go to www.noellemarie.com/school-for-dreamers to learn more and sign up. I would be honored to have you join our 2nd Course in the School, *Activate Your Power and Launch Your DREAM Business.*

Let's go on this journey together, of learning how we can fully unleash and tap into the unlimited power that is just WAITING to be awakened and activated from deep within us.

Trust me, there is a much more powerful version of YOU just LONGING to break through and change the world.

Are you ready to let that Powerful Person -- *the real you* -- OUT?

Then this magical book was written JUST for you.

Chapter 1

The Power of VISION

Fully Embrace the Highest Vision of You

All of the greatest, most productive, successful actions in my career have been a *direct* result of seeing, feeling, and embracing an enticing, thrilling vision of my Highest Self. I FEEL who I am -- the ME from the future -- I see and know that I AM that person I've always dreamed of being. I picture myself leading a huge team of people, singing at Carnegie Hall, living my dream as an inspirational world leader of awakening, and I feel the ecstasy of actually *being* that person. And from that powerful exciting vision, the energy and desire for the next step in my career ALWAYS flows easily to me, and then I effortlessly, joyfully *act* on it.

It's magical.

It never fails.

In fact, this practice is so reliable and powerful, I'm absolutely amazed that more people have not discovered this secret.

Why do you think that is?

Why don't more people realize that they can just FEEL who they are, and let all their actions flow out of this feeling, magically and effortlessly?

Maybe it's because we live in a world of striving and pushing.

And it just seems too simple.

You mean I can just DREAM? I can just FEEL who I am, and then everything will flow? I don't EVER have to strive or push?

I think it just seems TOO EASY for people, so they don't even give it a chance. And if you've spent a lifetime pushing and striving and working really hard for your money, it may surprise you to find out that there is a different way. So please feel free to keep striving if that's what you want. But I urge you to open your mind to the *possibility* that LIFE has provided a much simpler way for you to create and enjoy a purposeful, successful, abundant, powerful life.

I am living proof that there is another way. This joyful, easy approach to life is how I've walked into the life of my dreams in a VERY short period of time.

It's how in just 9 months I've written/published my first 2 books, recorded/released my first music album, launched the School for Dreamers, created *The Awaken Weekly* inspirational newsletter, started my own talk show (*Coffee Time with Noelle*), and launched my career as an inspirational speaker/singer to live audiences around the world.

I did all of this (and so much more) through absolutely NO striving or pushing.

No willpower.

Just fun, ecstatic DREAMING and VISIONING.

I did this by meeting and feeling this vision of my Highest Self every day. This is TRUTH. This is my personal, real, recent experience.

If I can do it this way, then so can you!

Clothe Yourself in the Highest Vision of You EVERY SINGLE DAY

I'm gonna let you in on a little secret, and it's slightly embarrassing. You're not gonna believe this. I promise you, this is the God-honest truth.

This morning when I came to my computer to continue writing this chapter, I felt numb.

I felt uninspired.

I knew I wanted to write the next section in this chapter. But I had no idea what to write.

It felt horrible.

So I closed my computer, and started writing about my feelings in my sacred space -- my journal.

In my journal, I can meet myself exactly where I am --
there's no thought of form, no outline to follow, no plan, no
structure -- just free-flowing thought. It's my daily therapy,
my connection with myself, my joy and delight.

And sure enough, as soon as I started writing and felt that
sense of surrender to Spirit, of letting go, I realized:

*OMG! I'm writing this chapter on how you need to feel your
Highest Self DAILY, and I haven't done that for myself yet
today. Hahahaha. Really?*

You see, I fell into the trap of thinking that my ecstatic
visions and feelings of myself from *yesterday* would carry
over to this morning.

But that's not how it works.

We must renew this vision of ourselves every morning of
every day.

There is a fresh vision of YOU that Life wants to give you,
every single day.

There are no carry-overs.

And there is *purpose* in this.

This dependency on Spirit is what keeps us surrendered.

It keeps us centered.

It keeps us focused on what's real.

It keeps us aligned and plugged-in to Source.

I seriously can't believe, after all these years of practice, that on the very day I'm writing about how to clothe yourself in the highest vision of you, that I forgot to do it for myself. I'm laughing out loud right now!

So I'm gonna share with you what I JUST wrote in my journal, which set me free and infused me with the ecstatic energy I'm feeling right now to continue writing this very chapter:

Tuesday, Oct. 6, 2015   9:30am

I felt the desire to move forward with my book this morning, and I opened my computer here in Starbucks, sipping my Americano, and

BAM – completely STUCK.

No inspiration.

No energy.

NOTHING.

Ugh.

So what is my chapter about?

It's about embracing the Highest Vision of me.

So maybe that's exactly what I need to do.

The writing has to be inspired or else it will be worthless.

I'm not just gonna force myself to type.

So I let it go, and I release myself to FEEL who I am.

I can't ride on the feelings I had yesterday.

I must cultivate them RIGHT NOW.

In THIS moment is where the power is.

So who am I?

What is the highest vision I can feel right now?

I am a writer. A book author -- internationally known.

I have several books on the NY Times Best Sellers List. People all over the world are reading my books and changing their lives as a result. People talk about me like they do about Elizabeth Gilbert, Wayne Dyer, and Eckhart Tolle. I am featured on talk shows like Super Soul Sunday, Marie Forleo, and the Today Show. I do book signings at big bookstores like Barnes and Noble, and the line of eager people wraps all around the store and around the block outside. The energy is palpable – excitement, anticipation, joy, inspiration. I feel the intense love for my fans as I sign their copies of my book and hug them. There is love and gratitude and tears in their eyes. They tell me how this book has changed their lives, and I feel my heart SWELL with joy and gratitude that I get to be a part of this awakening on the planet. I feel powerful, confident, strong, and alive. And most of all, I feel encompassed in LOVE. This is my heaven.

So this is an example of how to envision your Highest Self so you can FEEL who you really are.

What happened as soon as I went into this vision of my future self?

I felt JOY, ENERGY, and INSPIRATION.

And I couldn't WAIT to open my computer again and start writing.

This is how it works!

At least this is how it works for ME.

You can find your own way.

I spent most of my adult life with my imagination lying completely dormant. I focused on the world of reality, pragmatism, plans, and rules.

But in the past 7 years since my spiritual awakening, I've learned that the greatest power we possess is in our imagination. We can literally DREAM our visions into reality.

I'm sure I fully embraced my powers of imagination as a little girl, but somewhere along the way I stopped dreaming.

Now that I've retrained my brain to do this and I practice this every day, it's become easy and fun.

DREAMING is now my favorite thing to do!

So if I can do this, you can too.

The Power is in the FEELING

The KEY to this daily envisioning is in the FEELING. Choose whatever vision helps you to most fully, vibrantly, ecstatically FEEL who you really want to be, which is who you really ARE.

It's the power of the FEELING that draws your destiny to you.

So don't approach this like a sterile exercise. Find for yourself whatever allows you to feel amazing about yourself and your future. You must learn to LOVE this process, or else you won't be inspired to do it every day.

Don't Avoid Your Dark Emotions –

Embrace Them!

My mode of finding myself and meeting myself changes from day to day -- it's not a formula, and it's always fresh and new. Some days -- actually a LOT of days -- the way to find my Highest Self is by focusing on the blocks to my joy. If I'm feeling depressed or heavy or sad about something, I start there. If I'm feeling anxious, I start there. You must meet yourself exactly where you are, in order to uncover your joy.

Joy is not a band-aid or a mask, it's WHO you are at your core.

So sometimes, and maybe lots of times, the answer to finding your joyful vision and feeling of who you are is by entering into the darkness of your thoughts, so you can reach your true center. Whatever you are feeling in THIS moment is where you need to start. Your current emotions in this moment are the key to accessing your joy.

> Powerful people aren't afraid to FEEL. They know that great power comes from embracing EVERY human emotion: anger, pain, fear, passion, joy, and love.

Meet yourself EXACTLY where you are.

No judgment, no censoring. Let yourself be human. Let yourself feel. This is the key to reaching yourself.

The Power of Movies

Other than journaling, watching movies is my main way of cultivating ecstatic feelings about who I am. When I watch the right kind of movie, I feel my future self STRONGLY.

Most of the time, the movie has some element that specifically relates to my unique destiny. For instance, the movie *Jobs* greatly inspires me every time I watch it because I identify with many facets of Steve Jobs' journey and personality. His confidence, vision, and leadership. His disregard for rules. His commitment to originality, to breaking out of the box of societal norms. His dedication to his gigantic ultimate vision, despite any circumstances to the contrary. His unashamed boldness.

Movies like this also help me to step outside of my life and see it from a much bigger perspective. As I watch Jobs' company start with no money, in his garage and then materialize into one of the biggest, most successful companies in the world, I know I can do that too. I can look at the point in my life where I am currently, and relate it where Steve Jobs once was in his garage. I can step outside my life and feel that I'm just in a movie of my own. The future huge success of my own career is just as real as my current modest success. It's all a part of the movie.

So as I watch this movie, I feel my future self. I don't identify with everything about Steve Jobs, of course. I'm also very different than he was. But there's enough resonance there to completely inspire me on my journey. When I watch this movie, I feel ECSTATIC about who I am. I feel limitless. And I KNOW that I can be as successful as I want to be.

So don't disregard dreaming and movies as a waste of time.

Dreaming is the most productive thing you can POSSIBLY do with your time.

Find what works for you.

Maybe for you it's reading biographies or fiction. Maybe it's hiking, being outside in nature. Maybe it's meditating. Maybe it's sewing, or playing the piano or listening to incredible music.

Anything can be a catalyst for feeling who you are. Find a way that works for you. Find a way that *excites* you. Find something that you love to do so much that you will not WANT to skip a day. It shouldn't feel like a chore.

It should feel like your most favorite time of day.

The time of day when you get to meet your Highest Self.

The time of day when you get to REMEMBER who you really are.

The time of day when you get to step outside of your current circumstances and realize that you are just in the middle of your amazing life movie.

This is the time of day you LIVE for.

I urge you with everything in me, find a way to meet your Highest Self every day, and your entire life will change.

You will start to become that amazing person.

You will draw to you everything that is meant for your unique destiny. You will magnetize the perfect people, resources, and inspiration needed to fulfill that ultimate vision of who you are and what you were meant to do on this earth.

I only just Begun

So much a part of me.

Room to grow.

25

Dreaming of the highest vision of YOU is the most important work you can possibly do with this day.

And the really good news?

It's also the most enjoyable thing you can possibly do with this day!

Live from the End

It is beyond my comprehension and wildest dreams that I have already launched a SCHOOL. I have successfully built the School for Dreamers, an online school of personal transformation and spiritual awakening which is changing lives around the world.

I look around now, since launching the School, and see that these online courses are all the rage. I had no idea. The inspiration and idea to do this came about very organically, and with no thoughts of what I SHOULD do, or of copying what any other leaders are doing.

I look at where I am now, a leader in this spiritual awakening on our planet, a spiritual teacher and life coach, an author, a founder of a school, and I think, "How did this happen to me, so FAST?!" I've had the School for Dreamers vision for several years now, but if you had asked me WHEN I thought this would happen in my life time-line, I would have said it would be in a later season of life, when I'm in my 70s or 80s, after a lifetime of experience and wisdom, after traveling the world with Vince, when I have a LOT more wisdom to share than I do now.

I would have PEED my pants if you had told me that I would launch the school at age 36.

WHAT?!

And YET, this is the reality I'm living. I live in a van, and I've launched this school that is changing people's lives, while living in this tiny home.

How did this big dream happen so fast? I'll tell you EXACTLY how it happened, because I remember the moment as CLEAR as day.

It was February 19, just a couple of weeks after moving into the van, and I was letting myself have a full day of journaling and dreaming. I had been in a time of craziness with the move into our new tiny home and my YouTube channel exploding, and I felt a little disconnected from myself, so I decided to take a full day to reconnect.

I let myself DREAM.

I let go of all the TO DOs, all the little details of my life, and I reconnected with the BIG VISION.

I let myself FEEL what it would feel like to already BE that famous, wealthy person I know I will be someday.

What would it FEEL like to have a reach like Oprah, like Taylor Swift -- someone THAT well-known on the earth, someone that wealthy. How would I FEEL today? And I let myself feel that Highest Self. Here is what I wrote in my journal that day:

> *How does a wealthy, famous, WORLD LEADER of JOY act?*
>
> *She GIVES FREELY and RECEIVES FREELY.*
>
> *How FULLY can I EMBRACE THIS DESTINY?*
>
> *How FULLY can I CLOTHE MYSELF in this reality?*
>
> *HOW FULLY can I IGNORE EVERY circumstance that points me to a lower reality?*
>
> *Give what I HAVE to GIVE.*
>
> *If I ALREADY AM that HIGHEST VERSION of myself – OUTSIDE of Time – how would I LIVE?*
>
> *If there is NOTHING I lack, how would I act?*
>
> *What would I give?*
>
> *What would I do?*
>
> *SING, SPEAK, WRITE, GIVE.*
>
> *No LIMITS!!*
>
> *I could offer a course that includes coaching, just to teach people everything I know about walking into your dreams.*

And there it was.

It didn't come from a place of

"How can I make money while I'm on the road?"

or

"What should I be doing to get me into the life of my dreams as a teacher?"

NO, it was *way more simple* than that.

It came from the powerful place of,

"Since I ALREADY AM a world-famous spiritual teacher and leader, what can I GIVE?"

And there it was.

Within one week of that inspirational moment, I fully launched the School -- with 7 students in that first group who were engaged and amazing.

I didn't have to do big launches or lots of advertising. The students just appeared, because they were ready to receive what I was ready to give.

It turns out, I didn't need to wait until I'm in my 70s to teach other dreamers how to really do this thing, because what qualifies me to help people NOW, at age 36, is the fact that I AM CURRENTLY LIVING my dream life, and I have learned how to hear my own voice and follow inspiration and joy in everything I do.

And more importantly, I know my power.

I have activated my power.

And when you KNOW your power and activate it, the resources of the Universe respond to you.

You become a powerful MAGNET and you attract everything you need for your mission on this earth: the people, the resources, the time, the energy and the inspirational ideas.

I want to teach you how to do the same, because inside of YOU is every answer you need for YOUR unique path.

Inside of YOU is power that is waiting to be activated so you can change the world.

And as you can see from my example, it starts with simply *living from the end.*

Imagine your ultimate vision of who you want to be, of what you want to be doing, and FEEL that vision strongly.

Trust me. It's powerful stuff, my friend.

You can do this. *Plug into The Source*

Close the Gap Between Your Current Circumstances and Your Ultimate Vision

At the moment I am sitting in Starbucks in Marquette, a beautiful city in northern Michigan which sits right on Lake Superior. I wanted to find a city on the lake where I would be able to settle in for a couple of weeks and write this book. And it's so perfect! It's autumn right now (my all-time favorite season), the leaves are all spectacular vibrant colors, and the dark blue of the lake is deeply soothing. It's a perfect place to settle in and dig fully into this book and the concurrent 2nd course in the School.

On the drive here yesterday, as I was anticipating that I would be delving deeper into a full writing schedule upon arriving in this city, I started processing my emotions. I was noticing a lack of desire for writing, a certain block in my emotions, and so I let myself feel it.

I met myself right where I was -- no judgment, no censoring, no pressure.

And as I journaled I uncovered some *pain* I was feeling that was dampening my sense of energy and joy about the creating process.

You see, there is a gap I feel between where the School for Dreamers currently is and where I would like it to be.

We have a handful of students every month who take the first 10-week course that I've created, *Bliss Beyond Belief: The Journey Out of Pain Into Your Highest Destiny*, and the results and feedback are off-the-charts amazing.

It's definitely changing lives.

And of course I'm SO happy about that. In just a few short months since its launching we are already making enough of a profit from the School that it is our main source of income and is paying most of our expenses right now. Lots to celebrate here! It's incredible!

However, I feel the gap.

I want MORE students.

I want to see this thing EXPLODE.

I want to feel more excitement from more students, more total engagement.

I want to see the students lining up to learn from me, eager to implement everything I teach.

So here is what I wrote in my journal yesterday:

> *Let's be honest, I'm not excited about this book right now.*
>
> *I'm not excited about ANYTHING right now.*
>
> *But I can feel my ecstatic joy – just around the corner.*
>
> *I will uncover you.*
>
> *I will not leave this journal until I find you, my joy.*
>
> *What is one thing that would make me ecstatic today?*
>
> *People. Students. My tribe.*
>
> *How would it feel to have students lining up to learn from me?*
>
> *Students READY and DYING to receive and implement everything I'm offering?*
>
> *THAT would make me extremely happy.*

I got a pang of sadness the other day because I was connecting deeper with one of my fans and she sent me the site of her "master teacher" and wanted to share her excitement with me about what she had found.

I looked at the website, and felt SAD.

Cuz it's very similar to what I want to be doing, and AM doing, but it's on a much larger scale, much further along than I am. So I got depressed.

Wow I'm really touching on something here.

I can feel I hit the pain.

This pain, this GAP I feel -- this is what's blocking me from feeling energized about this next course and book. I want to feel that there are hundreds of eager students out there who can't WAIT to read my next book, take my course, and pay good money for it.

And, right now, in the physical manifested realm, I'm not seeing that.

And so the gap between what I SEE and where I WANT to be, is BIG.

So how do I close the gap?

By IGNORING that there is one.

> Powerful people pay no attention to current circumstances that don't line up with their vision. Their eyes are set like laser beams on their dream life and purpose.

I must FOCUS ALL my imaginative power on FEELING what it will feel like to have thousands of people flooding the website, enrolling in the School. Email after email from people asking about the 2nd course, DYING to take it and READY to do so.

And just as I start thinking this, of course the natural human reaction is to think of a specific detail (like improving my website) that will allow me to reach these people better.

But at this point it is CRITICAL to focus ONLY on the feeling of ALREADY having it.

The powerful force, the magnetic power of this ecstatic feeling will effortlessly draw to me energy for every perfect action I need to take.

The power is in the unseen realm, so don't start jumping into the physical realm of action, Noelle.

Stay where the POWER is, and everything will materialize from the inside out, easily and joyfully.

And BAM! Here in the midst of surrender and writing about how I'm not excited about my book, I not only uncovered the BLOCK to my joy, I actually have continued writing my book, without knowing it. Amazing.

So right now, I embrace the FEELING of my tribe -- of thousands of engaged, ready to pay, eager to learn, dying to change their lives students who are hanging on every word I write and every teaching video I record.

They are flocking to us in the hundreds every day.

We have to hire an executive assistant because administratively it's blown up.

I feel the enthusiastic energy and hunger of all these students. They finish one course and can't WAIT for the next one. They are changing their lives. We have big profiles and testimonies of them on the website. Testimony after testimony of real people with real lasting change. We receive big donations for the scholarship fund. As we travel the country, there are thousands of students who can't wait to meet me in person and attend my workshops and conferences.

My job is to DREAM and CREATE. Don't worry about marketing. Marketing happens effortlessly as you focus on being FULLY YOU.

Imagine: A world out there waiting for you.

It's inevitable. It's coming. And you can just ENJOY it as if it's already here. TV talk show interviews, hotels, big speaking gigs -- AH! Don't forget what you WANT, Noelle! You want ALL of that!

> Powerful people know when to REST and when to ACT. They don't strive or push. They know that all action is easy and effortless as they rest in WHO THEY ARE.

Let it come.

Let it ALL come.

I am ready. I am ALREADY that person. A big team working for me. Big speaking invites flooding in. YES!

So as always, it's vitally important that as I see what I could DO next, and even as I make plans for what I WILL possibly do next, that I REST in the big vision.

I must always CLOTHE myself with the BIGGEST vision FIRST.

My joy and energy is NEVER in the details of the next step, but always in the ECSTASY of the ultimate vision of my life.

I remember church 36 trying to get 10% from someone on SS. She barely made it on her own

my Grandma being told she was a proper + told not to come to church.

There is a lot of treasure for you here in this journal entry -- about living from the end, meeting yourself where you are, closing the gap between where you are and where you want to be, and finally the VERY important piece of truth that it never works to focus on the specifics of HOW you will get to your vision or what you will actually DO next to accomplish your dream.

The key to moving towards your dream life is to REST in the vision and let the energy for action flow to you naturally and easily.

I have found that when it's time to ACT on a vision, the energy of that kind of inspiration is so strong, it's as if I can't NOT act on it.

It should not feel like pushing or striving at all.

When it's time to act you *will* need to walk yourself through some fear, but there is never any need to push yourself off the cliff.

Meet yourself where you are, and the perfect energy to act will come, in the perfect time.

Rest in the vision.

It's enough.

So as I uncovered this pain of the gap, I transformed the pain into PASSION and energy for my book and course.

I started actually FEELING the joy of what it will be like to have thousands of students flocking to my school.

And the feeling of that vision is so real to me now, it's ALL I see.

And as I pay no attention to my current circumstances in the School (other than gratitude for the amazing students I already have, of course), I feel powerful and joyful.

I feel inspired.

I know that the reality of huge numbers of hungry students is just a matter of time.

And because I am ultimately OUTSIDE of time, I can close that gap NOW by entering into that vision of my ultimate reality.

So I urge you to do the same.

As you uncover sadness about the gap between where you are and where you want to be -- CLOSE it.

Close the gap by ignoring that there is one.

✗ Focus so strongly on the fact that your ultimate desire *will be fulfilled*.

Focus intensely on the ultimate circumstances you want, so much so, that it's all you feel.

As you feel it, it will be drawn to you.

It will be drawn to you in the form of energy for the next step, inspiration, people, resources, opportunities -- EVERYTHING you need to reach that ultimate vision will come to you, easily.

Don't strive. Just let it come.

Learn to act fully from your joyful energy, from the vision, NOT from pushing or willpower.

As you do this, your destiny will accelerate, and you will feel like you're just along for the ride, instead of trying to *make* something happen.

You will feel like you're in the zone, in the flow, and everything will be organic and easy.

This is the key to unleashing your limitless power.

Clothe yourself in that highest vision of YOU every single day.

In fact, if you are feeling very inspired and insanely enthused about this, I urge you to do something crazy, right now.

Warning: This is only if you're ready to really activate your power.

This is only if you're ready to actually walk into that life of your dreams.

If that feels like you right now, then ask yourself the following, out loud:

"How FULLY could I clothe myself in the highest, most outrageous vision of ME, today?

How FULLY and completely could I wrap myself up in this amazing feeling of who I ultimately want to be, right now?

How FULLY could I choose to live in this feeling, today and every day?"

I DARE you.

Chapter 2

The Power WITHIN

Everything You Need and Want Is Within You

I am nearing the end of my 4th year of working full-time in my dream life. When I started this journey -- when I took that leap of leaving the corporate world -- I did it because I was following my heart. I didn't know exactly what my path would look like or exactly what I would do, but I knew I had to listen to the deep cry in my heart to find my highest destiny, to go after my dreams -- as scary and unknown as the journey seemed.

At the time that I quit my job, Vince had recently been laid off from his corporate IT job. We had a mortgage and credit card debt and student loans and lots of other bills and I was attending ministry school to learn how to find myself. We had no plan of how we would support ourselves financially, considering his small unemployment income and my complete LACK of income.

But here's the thing: The pain of living a life that didn't fulfill my deepest longings -- a life where I had to numb my desires just to get through the day, a life of being someone I didn't really want to be -- when the pain of all that got stronger than my fear of the unknown, I jumped. I took the leap. I jumped off the cliff. And Vince supported that jump. We took the leap together.

I will never forget the day, several months before the JUMP, when I FIRST told Vince that I wanted to quit my job.

He erupted in some very strong emotions. I knew it was fear.

And I don't blame him -- it was CRAZY to think I would quit my good job with great benefits when he was unemployed.

So I let it go.

And I worked out a plan with my boss to have a flexible schedule in which I would go to my ministry school during the day, and work during the early morning and evening hours.

A few weeks into that crazy schedule when I was hardly ever home and had to cram my homework into the late evening hours, Vince told me he wanted to talk. I saw the look on his face, and I knew it was serious. But he looked tranquil, serene, calm. I was exhausted, but suddenly a PEACE came over me, just looking at him.

We sat on the couch, and he said to me, "Sweetie, I don't know HOW it's gonna work, but I realize now that I don't need to know how. I see you working these crazy hours and then cramming in the most important part of your day, your school work, when you're at the end of your energy, and I can't watch you do this anymore. I know we're gonna be ok. You have to follow your heart. I just want you to know that I'm gonna support whatever you want to do. If you want to completely quit your job, I'm with you. Your dreams are too important to shove to the end of your day. God will take care of us."

And so we jumped. I gave a 2-month notice at work, and January 1, 2012 I began my life as a free agent. All my time was now free to follow my dreams, whatever that would look like.

And Life supported that jump.

You see, here's the thing:

When you make the most important decision you will ever make in your life -- the decision to follow your heart and your unique life path -- all the forces of the Universe come to your aid to support you.

You have a destiny on this earth, and when you align your life with that destiny -- no matter how illogical or crazy it may seem to our culture -- you are Divinely supported.

I'm not saying that money just falls out of the sky and everything instantly becomes perfect.

But everything SHIFTS, if you let it.

After we took that leap of faith, all kinds of shifts happened.

Instead of lots of money miraculously coming in to cover the bills and the mortgage, our *perspective* changed. As we stopped being ABLE to pay the mortgage, we discovered the idea to let it go and move into a school bus. We discovered a government plan for student loans called *Income-Based Repayment* that allowed our monthly payment to go to ZERO, based on our income.

THESE were the types of miracles that Life brought to us. We were always provided for.

And we were HAPPY!

It was ADVENTUROUS. We suddenly felt ALIVE.

> Powerful people are insanely HAPPY regardless of external circumstances.

And when I look at my life NOW, although it doesn't look exactly the way I thought it would (it's so much BETTER than I dreamed), I am utterly amazed at where this path has led me.

It has led me to an incredible discovery -- the thing deep down I've always been searching for -- it has led me to the discovery of a priceless treasure.

I have been journaling since I was 12, but it was always sporadic, up until 4 years ago. There is rarely a day when I don't journal now. It has become my daily delight, my deep and dependable connection to Spirit and to myself.

Recently I have seen the value in my journals. I always thought it was just fun, just for me, but now I've discovered that there is real treasure in my journals, so I've started digitizing them. I am in the middle of typing into my computer every word I've ever hand-written.

Little did I know, that this process would reveal deep and incredible mysteries -- ones that I can see now, simply because I'm looking at my life from a timeless perspective.

When you step outside of your life and take a good long look at it, you see things that you just can't see when you're living in your narrow daily reality.

The treasure I'm finding in these journals of mine, this magical journey of looking at my life as a whole, is having powerful results in my life.

I want to ATTEMPT to capture right now in words what this process is doing for me, but I know I won't be able to do it justice.

It's a magical feeling.

It's a sneaking suspicion,

a tantalizing truth,

an amazing reality.

It's like I'm walking on a beautiful path and I'm just about to turn the corner, and even before I get to the bend in the road, I can smell it, see it, feel it, hear it --

there are all these waves of colorful light beaming

from around the bend.

It's calling to me,

drawing me closer --

it's the knowledge that the glorious fragrance,

the faint but enticing melodies,

the glimpses of radiant light,

are not even a *fraction*

of the BEAUTIFUL SURPRISE that awaits me around the corner.

It's the knowledge that it's too good to be true,

that it's BETTER than I've conceived or dreamed of,

and that this GIFT,

this TREASURE,

this SURPRISE,

is in discovering:

ME.

Discovering that Noelle is HERE.

That everything I've dreamed of becoming has happened,

that WHO I AM is more thrilling,

more radiant, more exciting, more amazing,

than I ever dreamed possible.

It's the discovery of ME --

that I truly AM that person I've always dreamed of being.

That all I EVER NEEDED, the only thing I EVER LACKED,

the only thing that needed healing,

was my ability to SEE MYSELF.

That I've always been here:

fully radiant, fully magnificent, fully Divine.

And that these past 4 years of internal discovery, of excavating my internal landscape, have all been for ONE REASON:

For ME to SEE WHO I AM.

Because all I've ever needed was to SEE it for myself.

To see my radiance, to see *that I am the treasure.*

That I've never, ever, lacked ANYTHING.

You see, I thought my treasure would be about external success -- that it would be about giving concerts, speaking to live audiences and traveling around the world, books published, music albums and huge success.

And all of that is happening, and I'm amazed by it, for sure.

But I have found something SO MUCH GREATER than any external success could ever give me:

I have found that I already AM everything I've ever dreamed of -- I've always been here, but now I can SEE.

This ability to connect with ME, to feel WHO I really am, to find everything I need here, every single day, every moment of every day, is my treasure.

To feel this kind of deep satisfaction, deep peace and joy.

To know that I am plugged into Source, supported, loved, and adored.

To know my radiance and to be able to receive whatever guidance I need every moment,

NOT in some ethereal spiritual prayer practice,

but in the simple joy of journaling, of asking, of meeting myself where I am, listening to my voice and trusting my desire.

All of this is BEYOND any kind of joy ANY external success could ever give me.

And I found this joy, this incredible treasure inside me BEFORE any of the external success happened.

BEFORE my first book was read by anyone,

BEFORE my YouTube channel took off,

BEFORE we started traveling the world,

BEFORE I recorded an album,

BEFORE I built the School for Dreamers,

BEFORE I launched my live speaking career.

I found this treasure before any of that external stuff materialized.

And as I found the treasure of ME while sitting in Starbucks with endless hours of bliss ahead of me, no obligations pulling at me, no job to go to, no pressure of any kind (except the illusion of pressure from this egoic world we live in), I KNEW that I discovered the secret of Life.

That everything I had ever longed for was already here, inside me.

I just had to STOP long enough to be able to HEAR myself, to find myself, to learn to TRUST myself.

> Powerful people know how to hear their own voice clearly. They trust their desires no matter what anyone else thinks.

So what if YOU already have inside you everything you've ever dreamed of, and the only thing you're lacking, is the ability to truly SEE HOW AMAZING YOU ARE?

I'm here to tell you, it's not a matter of "What if?"-- it's the truth:

You have all the answers inside you.

You ARE the treasure you are seeking.

So look within.

Quiet all the voices that pull you in every other direction.

Listen to YOU.

That's where the true treasure is, that's where all the answers are.

Jesus said, "the Kingdom of God is within you." (Luke 17:21)

So why are you looking everywhere else?

> Powerful people know that their greatest treasure is found WITHIN.

Listen to your desires,

listen to your heart,

listen to the ache that calls to you in the night.

And maybe, just maybe, you will discover what you've always been searching for:

you will find the magnificent treasure, of YOU.

BEING vs. DOING

When I first chose to give myself the gift of TIME, I struggled daily with being able to receive it, to just ENJOY it.

I noticed almost immediately in those first few days of not working at a job that I felt this sense of *guilt*.

Here I was, endless hours ahead of me to enjoy, and everyone else was going to work.

Is this FAIR? Why do I get to sit here at a coffee shop while everyone else is headed off to work?

And so along with that sense of guilt came a sense of pressure.

To PRODUCE.

I thought, *If I produce something with my time, my free time will be justified. It will have VALUE. I need to produce something, quickly!*

And I immediately noticed all of these egoic thoughts rising to the surface, about how I thought that my time would only be VALUED if I produced something.

I realized I believed that I would only be seen as "successful," once I started making MONEY with my time.

And at the very least, I thought I needed to produce something measurable and concrete with my day -- at least write a blog, or a chapter in a book, or write a song -- at least have SOMETHING to show for my time.

Oh did I have a LOT to learn!!!

Little did I know, that it would take 2 years of DOING almost NOTHING except writing my journal, decompressing from those limiting beliefs, to get to the point of being able to accept and retrain my brain in these life-changing TRUTHs:

- All DOING flows out of BEING.
- Just your PRESENCE is enough -- it is invaluable.
- Your worth -- your insanely high value -- is not linked in ANY way whatsoever to what you PRODUCE physically, materially, or visibly.
- DREAMING is WAY more important than DOING.
- To be able to sit and ENJOY this moment, free from all thoughts of producing or DOING, is the most important "work" you can EVER do.
- When you are in Spirit, in the zone, in the true flow of life, there is no difference between WORK and PLAY.
- Life is not measured by what you produce, but by how much you ENJOY every moment.

Once I started embracing these truths, letting go of the upside-down perspective in which this culture had trained me, I began experiencing deep peace.

I let go of thoughts about how I thought *others* would be judging my life.

And when you just sit and journal for over 2 years, with no visible external output of any kind, it can be a difficult thing to let go of those cultural judgments about how you use your time!

But I am VERY proud and grateful to say, that I did it.

During our year of living in the school bus in 2013, I arrived at the point of total acceptance that I was highly valuable and worthy as a person, regardless of anything I DID with my time.

And the crazy miracle that happens when you accept that truth, is that it sets you FREE to actually produce something with your time!

I embraced myself and my PRESENCE as a valued treasure, completely separate from all output, which released me to become the creative person I had always been.

I had always been creative -- we ALL are -- but I blocked my creative power with all these pressured thoughts about what I SHOULD be doing with my time.

Releasing myself from that pressure at a DEEP level FREED me to just BE myself.

And it turns out, that BEING ME, is really cool.

I write books, I write songs, I record teaching videos, I DO all these really cool things.

But none of this output would have ever happened without FIRST releasing myself from the external pressure to produce.

You MUST begin letting go of the faulty conclusion (which, unfortunately, OOZES out of every inch of our American culture) that the value of your time is based on what you PRODUCE. And that in order to produce, you must WORK HARD.

It's just not true.

And anyone who has come close to death has realized this truth, most of the time too late.

According to the book *The Top Five Regrets of the Dying* by Bronnie Ware,

the NUMBER ONE regret of people on their death beds

is:

"I wish I'd had the courage to live a life true to myself, not the life others expected of me."

And also in the top five:

"I wish I hadn't worked so hard."

"I wish that I had let myself be happier."

I know it's not easy to embrace these truths in a culture that highly values being BUSY and working HARD.

Believe me, having spent 2 years sitting doing practically nothing with my time except internal excavation and dreaming, I can tell you that it requires insane courage to be at peace with just BEING.

And even though I am now creating amazing products with my time,

I STILL deal with this pressure,

I STILL have to tell myself every day –

You don't have to do anything today, Noelle.

You don't have to write that chapter in your book today to be valued. You're GOOD. You don't need to produce ANYTHING with this day in order for it to be a valuable day.

Your life is PRECIOUS and THIS is your day to enjoy.

And *boy* have we received criticism online for the way we live our lives.

It's a good thing I was offline during those 2 years I was "doing nothing."

Vince and I get insanely mean comments from people about how we live, *even though* I've now written books and started a school and recorded an album and all of that external success.

You see, anyone who still believes that you must go to a job you don't love in order to be a normal person,

anyone who still believes that you must make money every day in order to be a worthwhile member of society,

anyone who still believes that DOING is more important than BEING, is going to JUDGE you when you start to change your perspective.

Because if YOU start freeing yourself from these lies, it threatens the way THEY are living their life.

They are holding onto these beliefs about time and money SO strongly, they can't accept that someone would sit and journal all day, making no money, producing nothing *visible* with their time.

But secretly, deep down, they want to do just that.

They want to free themselves to live a life that's true to the longings deep within them.

And by making the choice to enjoy YOUR time on this earth, whatever that looks like for you, you are paving the way for others to do the same.

Just like I have paved the way for you.

I'm on the other side now, so I can tell you it's worth it.

And I don't think it has to take 2 years of resting to get to the kind of powerful place I am today.

I think that if you can let go SOONER than I did, of the idea that your time is only valuable if you produce something, you will actually get to the place of creating something for the world, SOONER.

The MOMENT I truly accepted that I was OK without producing, I started creating. I was FREE.

And here is the even CRAZIER reality I was actually PRODUCING all along. I was BUILDING ME. And all of those journal entries I wrote in those long blissful hours at Starbucks, fighting for ME, fighting for the ability to accept myself right where I was – all of that was actually PRODUCING.

It's all this treasure in my journals that is now becoming my books. And it would be valuable even if it was never shared with the world. It's mine. It's deep and real and it's treasure. It's work. It's valuable creation.

So can you let go of the idea that time has to be measured at all?

Can you just embrace yourself where you are, and free yourself to ENJOY your life?

Can you let go of what you *think* others are thinking about you, and just give yourself permission to spend your time the way you WANT to?

I've found that the answer to finding true spiritual treasure, true creative treasure, true LIFE, is by asking myself, every moment,

"How can I FULLY enjoy THIS moment? What do I really WANT right now?"

If you can start asking yourself that question, and then free yourself, *value* yourself enough, to DO what you want -- even if it's sitting on your butt today watching a movie, reading a book or sitting with your journal, or going for a walk -- the most indulgent thing you can think of to do that will actually satisfy something deep within you – if you can do THAT, you are one BIG step closer to enjoying your life. You are one big step closer to the life you want.

Don't wait until your death bed to realize that most people are living their lives upside-down.

Turn your life right-side up and start to just ENJOY it.

Right now.

THIS is your moment to LIVE.

Don't wait until everything makes sense.

Don't wait until you have enough money.

Don't wait until you complete that last commitment or obligation.

If you wait until the circumstances are perfect, you'll just keep waiting for the *next* thing to happen.

You are the one who gets to CHOOSE to live your life the way you want. Right now.

What if you knew you had only one month left to live?

Think about it carefully.

What would you be able to let go of, if you had such a short time left on this earth?

THAT'S what you can let go of, right now.

The illusion of obligation is just that – an illusion. It's not real.

You get to choose how you spend this day, and every day.

You are FREE.

THIS is your moment to LIVE.

> Powerful people live fully in the NOW,
> knowing the present moment is all
> there is, and that it is MAGICAL,
> LIMITLESS and POWERFUL.

I end this chapter with a recent excerpt from my journal. At the time I wrote this journal entry I was staying in a one-room cabin on a solo retreat. I used this time alone to connect deeply with myself. In the magic of that quiet solitude in the mountains of New Mexico, I discovered a deep sense of the POWER of just BEING ME:

September 3, 2015

I want to CELEBRATE that I really feel DIFFERENT.

I have no doubts about who I am.

I just feel like I'm suddenly a very HIGH version of me.

I feel ECSTATIC about who I am.

I don't need to add anything to what I'm doing.

Just the FACT that I've created a space for me to be me and that I KNOW MY POWER –

just THAT ENERGY ALONE is ENOUGH.

It's not about DOING more, it's about BEING more.

As I allow myself to BE ecstatically, fully me, I automatically enter a new realm, a magical reality.

This new energetic reality is ENOUGH.

It's SO POWERFUL, it magnetically attracts to me EVERYTHING I'm meant to have and do for my mission.

So the ONLY thought, the ONLY question, the ONLY intention I EVER need to focus on, is:

"How can I be more FULLY and FEARLESSLY ME in this moment?"

No matter what anyone else thinks, no matter what anyone else is doing.

The pure magnetic, powerful, vibrant energy of BEING ME is mind-blowing and limitless in its ability to change the world.

And THAT is the ecstasy I'm feeling.

THAT is the shift I'm experiencing.

The sheer BLISS of allowing myself

the freedom,

permission, and

SPACE

to BE WHO I AM

is enough to move mountains.

Chapter 3

The Power of FOCUS

Create Powerful Boundaries to

Live the Life You Want

I have always been strongly attracted to the idea of *focusing.*

Just the word *FOCUS* makes me excited.

Even as a teenager, I dreamed of the possibilities of directing my passion towards a single goal and rising to my potential.

I asked myself,

What would be possible for me if I really focused my energy?

How successful could I be if I was able to say NO to everything I don't want, and focus ONLY on what I DO want?

And I tried this several times, with moderate success.

At age 11, I started my own home-made whole-wheat bread business, taking orders at church, making all the bread myself, and delivering the loaves of yumminess to my customers on my bike. I made enough money one summer to take my brothers to an amusement park.

At age 14, I focused all of my passion into my violin-playing, and practiced up to 8 hours every day. I was really good, and my violin teacher (who was the principal violinist of the Duluth-Superior Symphony Orchestra), told me I was doing so well that I could be a fully paid member of the orchestra by the time I was 16, if I kept it up.

I didn't keep it up -- instead I had a minor nervous breakdown and stopped playing the violin altogether.

I sure was focused and very determined to succeed at the violin. So why didn't I carry on and rise to become a successful paid violinist?

The energy that was fueling my practicing was not coming from an unlimited Source. It was coming from a desire to prove my worth.

And that kind of energy that comes from the WILL, never lasts.

I am here to tell you, that I am currently in a focused life, tapped into true limitless energy straight from Spirit, and I am finally experiencing the true ecstasy of being able to bend all my energies into ONE direction. The external results are off the charts amazing, and the internal results? PURE BLISS.

It's what I dreamed of doing my entire life, and now it's REAL!

So in this chapter I intend to inspire you for what is possible and to give you the tools to do this yourself. You can unleash your hidden potential as you learn to tap into an unlimited Source of power and then focus this power towards living the life you really want. So let's learn how this works.

Tap Into an Unlimited Power Source

Before we even talk about focus, we have to address the issue of where your energy is coming from. Just as I've learned many times throughout my life, but starting at age 14 with my violin – the energy you are using to fuel your work must come from the right source, or it will never last.

It's very exciting at first to think that you can just DECIDE to focus, make a plan, do certain things every day and go for it.

That's the ego talking.

That's called *willpower.*

It will never last and it will not be fun for very long.

Believe me. Take it from someone who has been intrigued with personal transformation, success, and has read all the books on rising to your potential. I've taken willpower to the extremes.

You *can* do it with the energy of willpower. You can even achieve success that way.

But will you be happy and at peace? Will you be sustained for decades? Will the process be easy and joyful and effortless? Will you be sure that you are even on the right path for you?

Absolutely not.

The energy for your work -- for your life -- must originate with Spirit.

There is an easy way, a joyful way, an inspired way -- and all you have to do to make sure you are tapping into this unlimited, powerful energy, is by seeking WITHIN first.

Start your day, every day, by seeking inside you. Ask yourself where your heart is, where your desire is in THIS moment.

That's how you can get in touch with Spirit, with your Highest Self, with God -- and that's how you can make sure that you're on the right path for you, that you're tapping into the unlimited Source of power and energy.

All the work you do with your willpower alone is gonna be fruitless and worthless.

All the work you do that is fueled by the energy of inspiration and joy, will be lasting, eternal, invaluable, and powerful beyond measure.

Don't waste one moment of your life working with your willpower.

Surrender to Spirit, every moment of every day, and you will find true energy. It's magical!

There are two parts to learning how to focus. The first part is insanely easy, once you have achieved the second part.

Part 1:

FOCUS on one mission, on one main goal for your life. This is how you will spend most of your energy and your time.

Part 2:

Say NO to everything else.

Before we talk about saying NO to everything you don't want, let's talk about your mission. If the visioning in Chapter 1 was easy for you, then you have a pretty clear vision of where you want to be in your life.

If it wasn't easy, and you're not clear on what you want, that's ok. The more you surrender every day to Spirit and seek within, the more clear your ultimate vision will become. It's very exciting to not know for sure what you want, because then you are OPEN to receive exciting pictures of your life. You are OPEN to receive a better dream from Spirit than you have even allowed yourself to dream. So keep dreaming! Keep meeting yourself exactly where you are. Listen to your feelings. And keep surrendering. Your mission and destiny will become more and more clear, the more you create the space for YOU to be you.

So if you are not clear on your mission, then your decision of where to FOCUS your time and energy, is easy. You can make an intention to focus your time and energy on DREAMING. Or on getting to know yourself. Wherever you are on your journey, make an intention to focus on what you really want next. If you don't know who you are or what your dreams are, then I highly suggest making THAT your priority.

So once you know what your priority is, you can begin the process of creating a space in your life to focus on that mission.

How Are You Spending Your Most Valuable Resource?

Think of your time as a currency, like money. You are spending this currency every day.

Whether you realize it or not, YOU are choosing your life every day by every little decision you make about how you spend your time.

It's YOUR choice to get out of bed. It's YOUR choice to spend 30 minutes watching the news before work. It's YOUR choice to go to work. It's YOUR choice to go visit your mom after work. It's YOUR choice to do the dishes, to pay the mortgage, to go to church, to go for a walk, to watch a movie.

Your time is YOURS.

You don't know how much time you have left in this lifetime on the earth, but you are spending it like it's never gonna end.

It is absolutely true that you are an eternal limitless Spirit; however this particular life on earth is not eternal.

This will end.

You *will* pass away from this earth.

This TIME you are spending right now is precious.

It's WAY more precious than any money you have in the bank.

Take a moment, step outside of your life and take an inventory of how you are spending this invaluably precious resource.

When I decided to give myself the gift of having all my time free to pursue my heart's deepest desires, it was because I discovered this truth:

Time is way more valuable to me than money.

And pretty much anyone on their deathbed would agree with that.

So based on those terms and that perspective I have chosen, I can honestly say that I am the richest person on earth.

Why?

Because I have all my time available to me to live the life I want to live.

And I have learned to spend this resource in a way that is insanely fulfilling to me.

Sound good? Sound worth making some bold choices about how you are spending your time? I hope so.

If you do, you will join a special group of us who are turning the tide in our world about the value of time vs. money.

Don't get me wrong, I love money. It's awesome. I intend to have lots of it. But time will ALWAYS be more valuable to me than money.

And that's why I'm the richest person on earth.

What IF You Were Completely FREE from ALL Obligations?

If you're like me, just by reading about this idea of how you're spending your time, there are probably a few areas of your life in which you already KNOW you wish you weren't spending your time.

And you are probably saying to yourself,

I wish I didn't HAVE to go to that job.

I wish I didn't HAVE to talk to my mom every day.

But the truth is, you don't HAVE to do either of those things.

It's all your choice, my friend.

EVERYTHING you are doing with your time is your choice.

Once you face that, you can start to change it.

> Powerful people know their power.
> They take responsibility for life,
> knowing they are co-creators with God.

But before you start sweating with anxiety, thinking that you need to change everything in your life right now, just play a game with me.

It's called the "What IF" game.

Just think to yourself, or better yet, say out loud to yourself while letting yourself really FEEL it, the following questions:

What if I was free from my job?

What if I didn't have any family obligations whatsoever?

What if I didn't have any bills to pay?

What if I didn't have any commitments in my life at all?

What if I said NO to everything I don't want to do?

What if no one else cared what I did with my time?

What if I was given a clean slate, right now, and I could start over?

How free would I feel if I could really spend every moment of my day EXACTLY the way I want to?

This game only works if you stop your brain from all the resisting, limiting thoughts. You have to completely allow yourself to imagine that there are NO obligations in your life.

NONE.

Again, the power is in the FEELING.

FEEL that taste of freedom.

Feel it in your body.

What would it feel like to completely start over?

Now, just like any visioning or dreaming we do, the answer is *not* to start thinking of HOW you will get that feeling to manifest in your circumstances.

That's up to Spirit.

Your job is just to allow yourself (as often as possible) to FEEL what that freedom would be like. And I guarantee you, if you do that often and with deep emotion, the Universe will start bringing you the energy, direction, courage, and ideas to make different choices with your time.

And if you're thinking that any of this is SELFISH, you're dead wrong.

The most LOVING thing you can do for EVERYONE in your life and every other person on the earth is to live your truest, most free life.

Every decision you make towards freedom for *you*, is also a decision of freedom for everyone around you.

Just trust that.

Life will provide the perfect way to take care of everyone's needs, as you follow your own joy.

I'm not suggesting that you go out and quit your job, or divorce your spouse, or stop taking care of your kids, or stop calling your mom.

But as you begin to trust in the BEST way, as you begin to trust that Life has a way for you to actually be as free as you want to be, things will begin to change.

The Universe is *supporting* your search for freedom -- God wants freedom for you more than you do!

TRUST that.

As you FEEL the freedom first, you will begin to have courage to stop acting out of obligation.

You will identify facets of your life you can change right away, and it will feel AMAZING.

And sometimes when we make changes, people around us don't like it.

Because they're used to us acting a certain way.

And if WE change, it makes them feel like they might have to change, and that's scary for them.

But no matter how anyone reacts around you, just TRUST that making a joyful decision to follow your own bliss is ALWAYS ultimately GOOD for everyone around you.

How Important Is Your Happiness?

I am a very driven, focused person. I'm focused on my mission of awakening the world to joy. I'm focused on inspiring people like you to remember your magnificence and to follow those desires in your heart.

And MOST of all, I'm focused on being fully and fearlessly ME.

And over the course of the past year the results of my continued focus have come to beautiful fruition. It's been incredible to see people actually waking up and changing their lives because of my book, *Bliss Beyond Belief*, or because of the School for Dreamers.

But recently, I've discovered a whole new level of focus. And discovering this new insane level of laser-beam focus on my mission has increased my productivity ten-fold.

But even more importantly: my JOY in my life has expanded exponentially.

And THAT is why I'm so excited to share with you how I've been able to rise to this level of focus, so you can do it too.

Or at least, so you can know what's possible for you, whenever you're ready to implement it.

Because I'm gonna be honest with you, it requires *courage* to live the life you really want.

It requires courage to say no to everything and everyONE you don't want in your life.

So before we talk about these tough choices in my life that have allowed me to rise to this new level of joyful focus, I want you to ask yourself a question.

I want you to ask yourself how important your dreams are to you.

How important is your mission on this earth?

How important is it to you to live the life you really want?

How important is your happiness?

Are you confident that the world needs what you have to give?

I am.

I know, beyond a shadow of a doubt, how important YOU are.

I know, beyond a shadow of a doubt, how crucial it is to our world that you give yourself permission to live the life you were meant to live.

Because although it may feel greedy or selfish to think about spending your time in the *exact* way your deepest heart wants to spend it, it's actually not just about you.

It's about ALL of us.

Did you know that how you spend every moment of your day today, affects *me*?

It does. Because we're all connected. Every moment that you live in heaviness and obligational duty -- affects me and drags me down.

And every moment you live in freedom and bliss -- it lifts me up and empowers me.

WE need you to follow your bliss.

WE need you to say no to those unwanted obligations that steal your joy.

WE need you to live the life you came to earth to live.

Think of the most depressed, obligated person you know. The person who hates going to work and complains about it. How attractive and uplifting is that energy?

Now think of the most extravagantly happy person you know, if you know one. (If you don't, think of a child who hasn't learned to live in obligation yet.) The sheer abandon, joy, and carefree bliss of that person's energy is contagious! How attractive and uplifting is THAT energy?

So as you make these decisions to focus your time on what really matters to you, remember that simply by choosing happiness for yourself, you are uplifting the world. You will be an uplifting, energetic force for good in the world, simply by choosing to live the life you really want.

Where Are You Leaking Your Power?

So now to the fun part! Let's identify those areas of your life where your energy is being drained. Let's examine those places where your bucket is leaking, where your powerful life force is being wasted.

It's really very simple to discover where you are leaking your power.

Basically, it's anything you do that ends up stealing your joy.

Because the litmus test, ALWAYS, for whether we are on the right path for us, is whether the fruit of that action is PEACE, JOY, and LEVITY.

And when I say levity, I mean – it lifts you up in its lightness.

It's the opposite of heaviness.

Anything or anyone that leaves you feeling HEAVY, dragged down, uninspired, icky, depressed, lacking energy, self-condemning -- this is most likely an area where your bucket has some holes.

So our goal now is to seal up as many of those holes as we can. As you plug those holes in the bucket of your life, you automatically allow the flow of power to strengthen, like MAGIC.

Remember at the beginning of the chapter, I told you that focusing on what you want is actually the easy part, ONCE you say no to everything you don't want.

It's so true. Try it.

Try closing ONE thing in your life that is sucking your energy -- like constantly checking your Facebook newsfeed -- and you will immediately notice a surge of energy and power in your body and your emotions.

The more leaky places you seal up, the more energy and power you will feel being directed towards whatever you really want.

What if you could close up ALL the places your energy is leaking?

What could be possible for you if you focused ALL your energy towards the mission of being fully and fearlessly YOU?

I'll tell you, because I feel like right now in my life I'm pretty darn close to that.

Right now, after several years of focusing on letting go of obligation, I feel pretty damn free.

I feel all of my energy being directed toward my bliss, my mission, my purpose on this earth, while enjoying every moment.

And I'm here to tell you, it's worth EVERYTHING I've said no to.

> **Powerful people joyfully say NO to everything they don't want to do. They live from passion, not obligation.**

It's worth the uncomfortable talk with my boss, telling her I was quitting my job.

It's worth the firm boundaries I've drawn with my family.

It's worth letting go of my attachment to my credit score and letting go of my credit cards.

It's worth the fear of unfriending people on Facebook.

It's worth the judgment I've received for living in a van and not working at a "normal" job.

It's worth saying no to social norms of all kinds that make me seem like an alien on my own planet.

It's insanely worth EVERYTHING I've said NO to.

Because the life I have now, where ALL MY TIME and energy are FREE to flow towards

ONE MISSION,

ONE AIM,

ONE PURPOSE

(being fully me),

is SO incredibly, off-the-charts insanely ecstatically AMAZING.

I can't describe to you in words how incredible it feels, after a lifetime of people-pleasing, to enter a world where I can do what I want to do and be fully who I am.

SHEER.

BLISS.

So that's a lot of big stuff I've done -- quitting my job, drawing firm boundaries with my family, letting go of my big house and moving into a van -- but what about the smaller stuff?

I guarantee you that some of the smaller stuff you could do right now, will give you strength for the bigger stuff.

That's what I did. When I was still working in the corporate world, I started getting up 2 hours early and going to Starbucks to journal before heading off to work.

I used this precious early morning time to dream about what it would be like to not have to go to a job at all.

And eventually, those 2 hours of my day became so enjoyable and fulfilling, I realized I would give ANYTHING to expand that time to become my whole life.

And that's EXACTLY what happened.

Can you believe my life now?!?

I actually get to travel all over the country, sit at coffee shops, hours on end, just dreaming and writing, all day every day.

So what's one small choice you could make today, that would move you closer to your dream life?

Give your BEST energy to what you REALLY want, and it will automatically start to expand for you.

And if you are inspired, say NO to something that is stealing your energy.

And the power will start to flow in ways you never imagined possible.

Creating Powerful Boundaries in Relationships

Powerful people fiercely guard their heart. They only allow people who UPLIFT them into their inner circle, regardless of the past, or family ties.

If I had to take a guess at the ONE area that is stealing most of your power and joy, I would guess that it's in your *relationships.*

The insane power that our relationships have to either uplift or diminish our energy is extravagantly HUGE.

If you want to live a life of bliss and purpose, you are going to have to be FIERCE about two things:

1) WHO you allow to be in your life

2) What level of ACCESS you allow each person to have to your heart

Drawing boundaries in relationships is going to require a variety of choices, and each relationship is different.

So for each person in your life, you need to ask yourself 2 questions:

1) Is this person enough of a positive energy force in my life to justify continuing the relationship?

And if the answer is YES, then:

2) What level of access to my heart do I want to give this person?

People are always changing and growing, and YOU are always changing and growing, so this process of guarding your heart and having good boundaries is always going to be changing. It's fluid, because people are fluid.

But I'm here to tell you, from deep personal experience and agonizing powerful practice, that closing the door to certain people in your life who are a total drain to your life force and your purpose on this earth, is going to be VITAL to your ability to live the life of your dreams.

Here's my story.

It was one year ago exactly, and I had moved into a time of FINALLY sharing my story with the world. I had posted YouTube videos of my story and I wanted to start blogging regularly about my journey out of religion, into Spirit. It was a rite of passage for me to write publicly about this. It was just something I was insanely inspired to do – to write boldly about my journey out of Christianity, into total freedom in Spirit.

But I noticed a block in my energy that was preventing me from feeling free to pour out my guts online.

Every time I went to post anything on my Facebook page, I noticed a handful of people coming up in my mind. I heard their voices of judgment in my head, and I couldn't banish the thoughts of what they might be thinking. Some of them were former teachers from my Christian college, some of them were family members, but all of them had a certain *hold* on me.

Whether their judgment was just in my mind, or whether it was real, is of no consequence. Their presence in my Facebook world affected my ability to feel free at a crucial time in my life when I was venturing out of my cocoon. And for a long time I just tried to battle it or to ignore it, thinking that it would be a cowardly, weak thing to do to unfriend them. Also, I just thought that it would be too mean. Drawing boundaries felt MEAN to me.

But as I talked it through with Vince, and did some research online, I started to realize that if I was gonna follow my bliss and my purpose on this earth, I was going to have to make some tough choices that felt uncomfortable. I realized that my ability to feel free on my Facebook page was VERY important. I realized that giving power to these certain people who weren't contributing anything positively to my life, and were really just ghosts of old relationships anyway, was just crazy. How could I let a few people from my past keep me from marching boldly into my future?

So I did the unthinkable.

I unfriended the one person in my family who had the biggest hold on me -- someone who had been blatantly unsupportive of my dreams and extremely critical -- someone whose presence made me feel small. And this was a close family member. It was gutsy. And my heart was RACING.

And do you know what happened after I hit that button?

I felt the BIGGEST surge of powerful life force COARSE through my veins. It felt like I was a superhero and I had just taken a big dose of superpower juice or something. It stood up taller. I felt more like ME. I felt FREE. I felt POWERFUL. I felt ALIVE. I felt JOY!!!!

And in that moment, I realized:

My life is important!

My mission is important!

It's not going to kill these people if I unfriend them. The WORST that could happen is that their feelings get hurt. And if that happens, and there's something REAL in this relationship, then they will write to me or call me and we will talk about it. And then we will move forward with something REAL.

But in the meantime, my only litmus test for whether to unfriend someone or not, is gonna be – "would unfriending this person make me feel MORE FREE to share my heart with the online world?"

So I went a little crazy. I even unfriended family members related to family members who were affecting me negatively.

And looking back, I probably could have been a little more conservative and just clicked "unfollow" instead of "unfriend", but ya know what?

I don't have any regrets.

Because it freed me.

And my life is WORTH being free.

And I know I probably hurt people, and maybe some of them are still hurt, but not one of those people has come to me, asking me why or wanting to talk about it. And that shows me what the relationships really are at this point.

So I created a space for myself to be FREE to share my heart with the world. I closed up places in my bucket that were leaking and draining my energy. And I entered the BEST year of my life. I blogged every single day for over 2 months, which led me to release my first book, which led me to move into a van and head out on tour, which led me to launch the School for Dreamers, which led me to start my talk show *Coffee Time with Noelle*, which led me to write this book you're reading right now.

And it all started with the courage to click *unfriend* on one person on Facebook.

It all started with creating a space for ME to feel SAFE to be ME.

And honestly, I would welcome any of those people I unfriended one year ago back on my Facebook page now, because I've become a powerful person. I'm no longer pulled by my past. I'm no longer afraid of judgment. But at the time, it was crucial for me to create a safe place online to venture out of my cocoon. And I'm so glad I did.

Which of your relationships comes to mind when you hear my story?

Creating a boundary in a relationship does not mean you have to *end* it. And it does not even mean you have to tell that person that you're creating a boundary. Sometimes it's just a matter of changing the level of access that person has to your heart.

Think of it like a security badge to a big bank. Your heart is the bank. Some people's badges have access to all levels of the building, to all the inner rooms and precious places with the gold and the treasure. And other badges only have access to the outer rooms. You decide the level of access to give each person. You decide whether to open up your deepest heart over coffee, to ask that person for advice, or whether to just exchange a few text messages and stick to impersonal updates.

"Above all else, guard your heart, for it is the wellspring of life."

These words from Proverbs (4:23) are legendary wisdom. As you give yourself permission to keep the treasure of your heart safe from people who will stomp all over it or from people who will simply drain you in their presence, you will rise to a new level of energy, power, and focus.

Give yourself the gift of space to BE who you are.

Give yourself the gift of saying NO to everything and everyONE who is distracting you, so you can begin to FOCUS all of your amazing power on your most important mission on this earth: being FULLY and FEARLESSLY YOU!

Chapter 4

The Power of ABUNDANCE

Unleash the Unlimited Abundance of You

What comes to mind for you when you see the words *abundance, wealth, success, and riches?*

For most people, these words are associated with MONEY.

And before you skip to the next chapter because you think this is gonna be one of those messages about realizing that "you don't need money to be happy" and "you should just be grateful for what you already have," keep reading.

Stick with me here.

Because I happen to LOVE money and I intend to have a lot of it in my lifetime.

There is nothing wrong with money itself. As a Divine Magnificent Precious Powerful Person, you deserve to live the life that you want, and if having lots of money is something you desire, then you absolutely can and should have it.

And in this chapter I am going to take you full circle through a money journey. My goal is that by the end of this chapter you will have a new perspective on money that will actually allow you to attract more of it into your life.

The best way to attract more of something, is to first LET IT GO.

So for the purposes of this lesson, would you try to imagine a world *without* money?

We live in a money world. Everything is focused on it, to the point that we can't even SEE all the ways that we are insanely rich.

To the point that people spend their most valuable resource -- their TIME -- working at a job they don't love just to make money for *later*.

Can you see the insanity of spending the best energy of your day, your life's precious hours, at a job that isn't in line with your destiny, just so ONE day you can retire and THEN start to enjoy your time?

In my mind, that's absolutely INSANE.

It doesn't make any sense to me whatsoever.

And yet millions of Americans are living that way. In this upside-down world we live in, people like me and Vince who have chosen to live in a van and do what we love with our time while we're young, are RIDICULED in our culture.

Why do you think some people hate what we're doing?

Why do you think I've been compared to Hitler and people send us death threats?

Why do you think some people get upset with me for going to Starbucks twice a day?

All we are doing is enjoying our lives, before the "normal" retirement age.

The general public HATES what we're doing, because they have bought into the lie that you MUST spend your life working at a normal job. But this is just a societal norm that so many people have chosen to believe in. There's nothing true or real about it, and Vince and I are proof of that.

We didn't wait to have a bunch of money in the bank to decide to be together full-time.

We just said to ourselves, "If we only had one year left to live on this earth, what would we do with our time?"

And so, with that idea in mind, we were able to remove *money* largely out of the equation, by valuing everything else in our lives MORE than money and stuff.

Here is the list of things we decided we valued more than anything else, including money:

- Being together full-time, neither of us having to work at a normal job
- Traveling
- Being able to fulfill our purpose on the earth
- Being able to be FULLY who we are, regardless of what anyone else thinks

And you would THINK that you need *money* for all of that, right?

Well, we noticed something magical start to happen when we gave priority to these dreams, and didn't let the *fear of not having enough money* stop us from doing this, right now.

On January 1, 2015 we made an intention that we would take off into a life of traveling by February 1, 2015. And we were not gonna worry about HOW this would happen. We just decided to move forward with it, regardless of any obstacles or fears. At the time, we were in an apartment, Vince was working at a full-time manufacturing job, and we had NO extra money in the bank. Like, NONE. We were living pay check to pay check, to the penny.

We decided to do everything we could do to prepare, and let the Universe take care of *how* we would have enough money for our dream life. We just didn't worry about the money part of it.

We made a list of everything we owned, and spent the entire month selling all of it on eBay and Craigslist. We still owned the school bus home that we had lived in during 2013, and we put that up for sale. We figured that by selling that, we could make enough money to buy a Sprinter van which was our dream vehicle to live in. But it was the middle of winter in Colorado and we didn't have high hopes that we'd be able to sell the bus before leaving.

So we made the intention that we would leave February 1, even if the bus didn't sell, and that we would just sleep in the back of our Honda CRV (compact SUV) until we were able to afford to buy a van to live in.

On January 1 Vince gave notice at his job. It was exciting and scary!

It was such an adventure, not knowing how we would afford everything, but just KNOWING that we would be supported by LIFE because we were following our destiny. It's what we knew we would be doing, if we had limited time left on the earth. Thinking from that perspective puts a fire in your belly to truly LIVE!

It was a crazy but VERY exciting month. And we saw miracles happen immediately that confirmed for us that we were on the right path for our lives. The first miracle happened through Facebook. I had just released my first book, *Bliss Beyond Belief*, and I had a small following (a few hundred people) on Facebook from my blog. I sent a message to 20 of my most engaged fans, telling them about our plan and that we would love to visit them on our tour out on the west coast. I mentioned that we wanted to eventually buy a Sprinter van to live in, but that until then we would just sleep in our car. I was full of enthusiasm and I didn't have a SINGLE thought about any of them helping us. I was just sharing my JOY about our adventure with them! I couldn't believe what happened next. One of these fans called me and told me that he was inspired to help us on our trip, and that he would like to contribute $5,000 so that we could stay in hotels for the first few months instead of having to sleep in our car.

WHAT?!?!?

Are you flipping kidding me? What is happening?

In THAT moment, I realized:

Life was never gonna be the same again.

> Powerful people easily attract every resource needed for their mission by simply BEING themselves.

Life was supporting us, simply because we had decided to follow our bliss. And when you make the decision to follow your destiny, without worrying about HOW it's gonna work out, you are Divinely supported. This is just how life works. And it's pretty magical, trust me.

The *next* miracle, was that we sold the bus, in the middle of winter, within days of leaving.

The *next* miracle, was that we found our dream home, within ONE week of being on the road. It was the EXACT Sprinter van we had dreamed of owning. And with the generous money gift from that fan, combined with the money from selling the school bus, within a week of being on the road we had enough money to buy our new home AND enough money to live for a few months of traveling.

And everything else has just been one big adventurous, abundant wild ride.

Our lives are INSANELY amazing -- miracle after miracle happens to us every day. Our businesses are growing, we have never been too cold or too hungry, we have traveled all over the country, we haven't had to work at a normal job this year, and we are SO INCREDIBLY HAPPY and FULFILLED!

Our lives are ABUNDANT in every way.

> Powerful people don't wait for HOW their dream will come true. They focus on the vision and start running towards it, knowing they are supported by Life.

Do you see how this works?

We didn't let the *fear of not having enough money* stop us from living the life we wanted, right NOW.

We didn't wait until we had a bunch of *money in the bank*.

We didn't wait until we had a *perfect plan* of what to do or where to go once we got on the road.

We didn't wait until we knew *how we would make money* on the road.

We didn't actually factor MONEY into the equation, at all.

And yet, MONEY is flowing to us.

We actually have more money to spend on things we love to do NOW (like going to movies and coffee shops) then we did when Vince was working at a job he didn't love and we lived in a nice big apartment.

Isn't that food for thought?

So here is what I've learned in my life so far about the nature of abundance. And this is not from any books I've read, this is straight from my recent personal experience. This is true knowledge, because I'm LIVING it. These aren't just principles to me, this is what's REAL.

Because I've read all the money books. I know all about the steps to follow to manifest money and all that jazz. But none of that ever worked for me. So take it from someone who's tried everything under the sun related to money. There is a magical way, and it involves one KEY factor:

TRUST.

> Powerful people TRUST
> the Universe to provide for
> everything in their lives.

In order to have everything you really want, including money, you must get to the place where you absolutely KNOW that you are Divinely supported. You must KNOW in every fiber of your being that you are supported by LIFE, by GOD, by the Universe.

Animals don't worry about what they're gonna wear or what they're gonna do for food next year.

They live in the moment and they know that nature will provide for them.

Vince and I are experiencing first hand every single day, that when you TRUST in the *importance* of your life and your mission, then you can TRUST that LIFE is supporting you as you follow that mission.

Our entire society is set up on the *opposite* of trust.

The fabric of our culture is resting on the very shaky attachment to the fear of what MIGHT happen. And that's just crazy.

If you can let go of the fear of not having enough money, and trust that you will be provided for completely, you are opening yourself up to RECEIVE.

The MAGIC of Learning to RECEIVE and ENJOY

In Chapter 2 I told you the story of when I first quit my corporate job and I struggled with being able to ENJOY all my free time. The basis of this struggle was that I was learning how to RECEIVE abundance. The abundance I had dreamed of, which I now HAD, was having all my time free to do what I wanted.

But I struggled to enjoy it.

I felt guilty that I got to have it and others didn't.

I felt obligated to spend it to help others or to do something with it that other people would approve of.

But the reality, was that I had all this time because I dreamed it, I asked for it, and now I just needed to learn to accept that I was WORTHY of enjoying the gift LIFE had given to me.

I was practicing my ability to receive.

So here's another BIG TRUTH about abundance in all forms, including money:

You will receive MORE of what you want as soon as you learn to FULLY ENJOY what you already have.

You see, LIFE IS ABUNDANT. There is NO LACK.

Life is not withholding anything from you.

It is the easiest thing in the WORLD for Life to flow millions of dollars into your bank account right now.

So why isn't the money there?

Is it because you haven't worked hard enough?

Is it because you haven't saved enough?

Is it because you haven't been frugal enough?

Absolutely not.

It is simply because:

Life won't give you what you're not ready to receive.

I guarantee you: there are NUMEROUS riches in your life right now that you are not fully enjoying -- which means you aren't allowing yourself to RECEIVE.

And so Life knows, in Its incredible wisdom, that you would actually be *burdened* by having more of what you THINK you want more of, because you already have so much of it that you're not enjoying. You have so much that has already been offered to you, and you are simply not receiving it. By not fully enjoying what you already have, you are sending the message to the Universe that you're not yet ready for more.

Think about it for a second.

You've been given a lot of time – 24 hours every day.

Are you *fully enjoying* your time?

Powerful people fully ENJOY their lives.
Their work is play and their play is work – there is no difference.

Remember what happened to my time, when I started fully enjoying 2 hours of it every day, in those early morning hours at Starbucks?

I was given MORE of my time free! In fact, I enjoyed those 2 hours SO fully -- I *received* those hours SO FULLY -- that LIFE knew I was ready to learn how to receive ALL my time free.

And that huge gift of time *was* a bit of a burden, at first. I struggled with guilt, I struggled to believe that I was worthy to just ENJOY all my time, when everyone else was running around working so hard.

But because I stuck with it, because I was COMMITTED to learn how to receive and fully enjoy all of that time, that's why not only do I STILL have all my time free, but VINCE has all his time free, and our time has actually EXPANDED. One day for us now feels full and glorious.

It's magical.

Time itself has a whole new meaning for me.

I'm in heaven.

And all because I am allowing myself to fully ENJOY it.

I'm not worried about what others think about how I spend my time.

I don't feel obligated to spend my time in ways I don't want to.

And I had a big revelation recently, about this journey of receiving and enjoying this abundance of time. I realized that now that I've learned how to enjoy TIME, I can apply these same principles to MONEY.

Just as it was a bit of a challenge at first when I received that huge abundance of time into my life 4 years ago, if I had received huge amounts money before I was ready for it, it would have overwhelmed me.

You've probably heard the stories of people who have won the lottery, and they go crazy with the stress. A lot of them end of bankrupt.

The lottery money actually became a burden, because they hadn't gone through the personal growth to be able to RECEIVE and ENJOY the gift of money and time.

So be assured that you are absolutely deserving of all the beautiful gifts this life has to offer, including time and money. But in order to allow more of these gifts into your life, you have to give yourself permission to enjoy what you already have.

Think about the gifts of time or money in your life that you could be enjoying more.

Are you spending all of your time and all of your money the way you really want to, or are you spending these resources out of obligation or fear?

Be assured that Life will not give you more time or money if you are trapped in obligation. Think about what would happen with MORE time and money, if you are already burdened by what you currently have?

It would destroy you.

You'd be stressed out of your mind.

> Powerful people know that Life is abundant, and so they FREELY receive and FREELY give, guided by JOY, not obligation.

So start today to attract more of what you want into your life, by thinking of ways you can enjoy what you already have. This isn't some super-spiritual technique to get you to stop wanting more, it's just the reality that Life is incredibly WISE and GOOD and won't burden you with something you're not ready for.

So if you want more time and money, get READY for it! Start sending the message to the Universe that you are ready for more, by enjoying and fully utilizing what you already have.

Ask yourself,

"How can I more fully and completely SAVOR and ENJOY all the TIME I already have in my life?"

And

"How can I more fully and completely SAVOR and ENJOY all the MONEY I already have in my life?"

Vince and I are already experiencing huge shifts with money. I've had to retrain my brain that it's not BAD to want it. I've learned that it's just another resource that Life wants me to enjoy. I've learned to stop giving it so much POWER.

Once you stop glorifying money as *better* than other types of abundance, you open yourself up to being able to enjoy it more, which makes you more ready to receive more of it.

And one way to let go of your attachment to money, to loosen the power it has over you, is to realize all the amazing stuff in your life that already makes you so abundant.

All the money in the world could not compare to knowing that I am living my purpose and making a huge difference in people's lives. I received an email from a precious fan named Daniel just this morning who has been touched by my first book, *Bliss Beyond Belief: The Journey Out of Pain Into Your Highest Destiny.*

Listen to these words that made my heart burst out of my chest with joy:

> *Reading your book for the third time and it's sinking in. I now realize that I've been doing life all wrong. It is all about finding out who I am and what I like. No people pleasing for me anymore or obligating myself*

to anyone for any reason. I can say a big NO now and feel good about it.

I've read a lot of books, yours just makes more sense and it's not complicated and it resonates with me.

To which I can't thank you enough.

I can now feel a sense of who I am and the wishes and dreams that I need to awaken Dan.

Your book has ignited a spark in my life that I needed.

All I was doing was surfing YouTube of living a more fulfilled life and there you were. And the more I watched the more I connected -- wow. It was more than just the nomadic living than I thought.

Way more.

Love and Hugs and Thanks

Daniel

Take it from me, there is no amount of any kind of money or gold or treasure on this earth that could compare to the ecstatic feeling of complete fulfillment I have from reading an email like this.

The deep fulfillment of knowing that I am inspiring others, that I am awakening others to live the life they really want to live -- the fulfillment of knowing that I am doing my purpose on this earth -- NOTHING can compare to the extravagant abundance of that.

> Powerful people have extravagant love for themselves and this naturally spills over to bless everyone who encounters them.

And the amazing thing is, as I follow my destiny all those other things like money and nice things and hotel rooms and eating out at nice restaurants -- all of that just follows big and full as a RESULT of learning to just enjoy my life and follow my bliss.

And when money comes as a *result* of loving your life, you can be sure that you will be able to receive it and enjoy it, not be burdened by it.

Here's the truth:

YOU are abundant.

YOU are limitless.

YOU are the treasure.

YOU are worthy of living the life you've imagined and longed for.

Give yourself permission to ENJOY your life, and all the abundance that Life has to offer will flood into your life so extravagantly and fully, your only challenge will be to learn how to *handle* all of the excitement.

Let yourself RECEIVE.

ENJOY.

It's all YOURS!

Chapter 5

The Power of BOLDNESS

Embrace Your Greatness

and

Boldly Share Yourself with the World

I have always greatly admired confident people. I always watched them from afar, as if they were in another class of human than I was. I secretly longed to be like them, but never really thought I had it in me. It felt as if I was made from different stuff. How could I ever be like these fascinating people? How could I ever be so bold, so comfortable in my skin, so free to *shine*? How could I ever magnetize others to follow me as I saw my heroes doing? How could I ever be so unapologetic, so confident in myself, so commanding and charismatic, so charming?

It just didn't feel *possible* for me. It felt like there was this huge chasm separating me from confident people. It seemed like I was destined to live out my life in longing and insecurity.

And yet, after I did my first full guest speaking gig at a church last month and felt myself radiating charisma and confidence, sharing myself boldly with a live audience, successfully inspiring them to follow me, freely SHINING, unapologetic, completely comfortable in my skin, unashamedly magnetizing everyone around me to a life of freedom and bliss, I had to face the facts:

I am now one of those confident people I have always admired from afar.

I had to FACE that fact, because there was a part of me that I now needed to let go of. I realized that in order to fully step into my power as a leader and mission-driven business-woman, I needed to let go of that girl who thought she would never be one of the "confident" ones.

I realized I had *become* a confident person, but I was still looking UP at myself from a lower level. I was looking at myself from across that chasm, as if it wasn't REALLY me. Others had been seeing the greatness in me, but I hadn't been able to fully accept it. And I realized that along with accepting greatness, means facing some fears.

There was a lot of *safety* in being a shy, insecure person.

And I realized it was time to let go of that lower view of myself I had always held onto.

It was time to FULLY embrace that I am a leader, that I am great and confident and that I am one of the fascinating, bold people I have always admired.

And in letting go of that old picture of myself -- that old grid through which I had always safely viewed the world -- I found myself on a scary but enticing, very exciting new level of POWER.

And THAT is what led me to write this book.

Feeling the ecstasy of this new level of power was SO inspiring, I couldn't NOT share it with you.

So here we are, at the chapter I've been DYING to write for you since the beginning this book idea came to me.

It's TIME to embrace your greatness, my friend.

It's time to embrace that you ARE one of those people you've always admired.

It's time to step up fully into your power.

I know it's scary, because I'm feeling it right along with you.

What does stepping into your power look like and why is it scary?

It looks like sharing yourself boldly and opening yourself up to criticism.

It looks like not waiting for others to promote you, but boldly sharing yourself and your gifts with childlike joy.

It looks like getting crazy clear about your specific mission and not modifying it or watering it down in order to avoid judgment.

It looks like boldly asking others for their participation and support.

It looks like sharing your story – vulnerable parts included.

And it's scary because it means you will be judged. You will not be hiding anymore. You will not be using excuses anymore. You will be in the spotlight. You will be exposed.

That's all the scary stuff, but here are the *results* of stepping into your power, which I can tell you with every fiber of my being makes it ALL WORTH IT:

- You will feel powerful
- You will become unattached to criticism and praise, which will make you feel invincible
- You will feel more joy and ecstasy than you ever knew possible
- You will experience the deep fulfillment of living your life purpose
- You will experience the deep fulfillment of inspiring others to live better lives
- You will have more resources -- time, money, people, and opportunities -- than you know what to do with
- You will be fully and fearlessly YOU
- You will *change the world!*

Are You Afraid of Your Greatness?

One thing that was keeping me attached to my insecure, lower view of myself, was this feeling like it wasn't *cool* to be really bold.

Almost like I didn't *deserve* greatness.

Deep down I had this fear that it was SELFISH to be a great, powerful person.

After that first speaking gig at a church, one of the pastors offered us her gorgeous mountaintop home outside of Boulder, Colorado while she and her husband were on vacation for ten days. It was insane abundance – hot tub, breath-taking views, expansive stillness, and a big beautiful house on a mountain which I had all to myself every morning.

On the first day of this mountain-top retreat I was feeling physically ill – I had contracted a flu virus, which was extremely rare for me. I hadn't been sick in years.

I knew I was going to receive some kind of direction or vision for my life – I could just FEEL it. The inspirational message I received that morning is one of the greatest treasures of my life. When I first read it out loud to Vince, I knew something had drastically changed within me. It's honestly a little scary sharing it with you, because it's very fresh and personal. But we are all connected, and so I know it's not just for me, it's for you too.

Here's what I felt Spirit saying to me (which of course I recorded in my journal):

> *I set you free, Noelle, to be as BIG as you want to be -- To be as BIG as you ARE!!!*
>
> *Don't LIMIT YOURSELF.*
>
> *Look at what has happened!*

You have become the inspirational, dynamic speaker/singer/author that you've always dreamed you could be!!

Don't LIMIT YOURSELF.

Stop thinking of what to DO next.

It's time to STOP and CELEBRATE!

This is your mountaintop to celebrate and FULLY EMBRACE the BIGNESS of WHO YOU ARE.

I've brought you to this mountaintop so you would be able to FEEL your MAGNIFICENCE.

You are tempted to rush forward without taking a step back and really SEEING WHO YOU HAVE BECOME.

I want you to completely let go of ALL THOUGHTS about what you will DO next.

You will only be able to see clearly what to DO, once you have SOAKED in WHO YOU HAVE BECOME.

You haven't drunk it in yet, and that's why the future feels cloudy. Once you DRINK DEEPLY of what has happened in you, there will be no doubts of what is next.

YOUR INSANE JOY will lead you clearly.

You are on a new level. Whenever I bring you to a new level, it is crucial to EXPLORE, to CELEBRATE, to

LOOK AROUND, because the VIEW is MUCH DIFFERENT from this higher level.

You must learn to SEE with new eyes.

This is why you got sick. Because you were tempted to keep running, to keep moving, without first STOPPING to simply CELEBRATE and RECEIVE and ENJOY the GIFT of this new reality you've entered. Your old paradigms won't work here. You are feeling your old self pulling strongly on you to keep operating from the old habits. But that won't work here.

You are a GREAT LEADER now.

You are a much higher version of you. You have new eyes, new confidence, new spiritual insight, new magnificence and leadership ability.

You are looking at your next possible steps from your old view of yourself.

That won't work.

From this new higher level, you are more powerful. But you must be AWARE of your power and learn how to use it.

Doors that were closed to you will now OPEN EASILY. There are so many open doors now, you can literally do anything you want.

But there is an EASY way, a JOYFUL WAY, an insanely MAGICAL WAY just for you.

And the ONLY WAY to know this way, is to SOAK, to SEE – to FULLY SEE WHO YOU ARE NOW.

You THINK you know, but you don't yet.

Once you fully SEE who you are, you will KNOW the WAY.

The ecstasy of who you are will activate your new power.

You are still looking UP at this new you, as if it's not you.

You're looking at other people from your old level. It's not gonna work to do that because you lose all your power when you do that.

You are BIGGER than this mountain you're sitting on. It's time to SEE WHO you REALLY ARE. You are the LEADER. Rules and limits don't apply to you. All the doors are OPEN.

That speaking engagement was Life's way of saying, "It's TIME, you are ready."

The veil has been lifted, Noelle. You are no longer hidden. Your POWER has been ACTIVATED. Do you realize what this means? The DOORS are OPEN to you.

If you knew how limitless your options were, you would not give away your power.

You are the LEADER.

It's TIME.

The WORLD needs you to LEAD.

Don't limit how big your reach can be NOW.

It's TIME. Don't you SEE?

Your thoughts must become ALIGNED with your identity and the bigness of this new level, in order to fully activate your power.

You can do ANYTHING you want to do.

I took a deep breath to let all of this soak in, and then I looked up.

And sure enough, right there on the microwave clock, was the time: 3:33 (my all-time favorite number that always lets me know that I'm tuned into Spirit and on the right track for my life).

This inspirational message continued, and I want you to receive this as a message straight from my heart for YOU, because whatever has been given to ME, is also for you, because we are all ONE!

Stop thinking that it is a disservice to the world for you to know your greatness.

On the contrary, the VERY BEST thing you can possibly do for the world is to embrace FULLY your insane GREATNESS and the BIGNESS of your leadership.

They NEED YOU to be the leader.

Where you are leading them?

To see their OWN greatness.

This is GOOD.

Be BOLD!

Be BIG!

Be CRAZY CONFIDENT.

Those who are afraid of their own greatness may be offended or angry, but those who are ready and hungry will RISE WITH YOU.

Let yourself RISE.

BE MORE, DO MORE, RECEIVE MORE than you've ever dared dream.

What are the limits you are seeing or feeling? Let them go!

There ARE NO LIMITS for you.

Think BIGGER.

CREATE. BUILD. EMPOWER. DECLARE. GIVE. RECEIVE. EMBOLDEN. SUPPORT. LAUNCH.

BE BOLDLY FULLY YOU!

> Powerful people KNOW WHO
> THEY ARE. They aren't
> ashamed to feel and know
> their MAGNIFICENCE.

I'm gonna be honest, that even as I write this now, it feels scary. Because embracing my greatness feels vulnerable. But if I don't embrace my own greatness, I won't be able to lead you into *yours*. So YES, it's scary and it feels very vulnerable when you first start declaring your magnificence and walking into your power. But if you want to live a life of purpose, of power, of changing the world like I do, then you're just going to have to accept the discomfort of stepping up to this leadership level.

And I think for me, personally, it mainly feels scary because every leader in the history of time has been fiercely judged. I've always been slightly protective of leaders when people judge them in my presence, probably because deep down I knew I was gonna be one someday. Whenever people bash President Obama or anyone in the spotlight – even famous movie stars or anyone in a leadership role, I always defend them. I don't care if you agree with what a leader is doing or not, in my opinion every leader deserves respect. It takes an insane amount of courage and character to be in the spotlight at all. Most people in this world are happy to sit back on their couches and judge what other people are doing. How easy is it to judge what a leader is doing, but what are YOU doing to change the world? At least a leader is doing something to make a difference, and that takes *guts*. And so ever since I was a little girl, I've had a special place in my heart for leaders who are judged. I've never understood how people can be so mean.

And yet now that I'm a leader and some of my worst fears have come true regarding being judged and criticized, I've come to accept WHY people judge, which helps me greatly in not getting offended and even being able to have compassion for those who judge me.

People who judge you for *shining*, are just afraid of their own greatness.

When you shine, you reflect their own greatness back to them, and they don't want to see that. They want to stay in the darkness, stay hidden, stay powerless, refuse to believe that they can do something great and powerful and meaningful in this world.

Mostly I protect myself from judgment by having Vince filter all the comments and emails that come to us online. But when one slips through and I feel that anger from someone just because I'm being myself, it helps greatly to understand *why* these people judge me. People who criticize me are just blind to their own greatness, so they definitely don't want to see mine.

And their blindness is not a reason for me to STOP shining, it's a reason for me to shine even brighter and more boldly.

Because I was once one of them.

I was blind.

I was afraid to shine.

And some leader (like I am now) kept shining, kept sharing, kept boldly radiating her light, so that when I was ready, I was able to see what was also possible for me.

So don't let the fear of judgment from a blind and hurting world keep you from shining your light, boldly and outrageously.

There is a tribe out there looking for you.

They are waiting for you to lead them out of the darkness of their own insecurity.

And the ONLY way they're going to see who *they* really are, is by seeing YOU shine.

So let go of the old grid.

Let go of the old picture of who you are.

Decide today to step into your power, into your TRUE identity.

You have never been weak, you just didn't know your power.

Let the ecstasy of who you are begin to activate your limitless power today.

Soak in it, revel in it, fully embrace the GREATNESS of you.

And then find a way to share yourself.

As you share YOU, others will begin to see themselves in you.

As you let your light shine, you will give others the permission to shine their own light.

I'm sharing myself boldly and vulnerably, in order to inspire you to do the same.

Share the real you.

Vulnerably.

Boldly.

Unapologetically.

Step into your power.

At the end of this lifetime on the earth I bet that you will not regret having stepped boldly into your power, but I know that you will DEFINITELY regret it if you don't.

So as you step out boldly and declare to the world who you are and what your mission is, keep in mind those who are hurting.

Those who are meant to find you.

Those who will be kept in the darkness if you don't shine your light.

Keep your eyes and heart focused like a laser-beam of love on your tribe, your true audience.

Focus on the ones who *need to see you shining.*

> Powerful people know that the world needs what they have to give.

Concentrate your passion on those who need to see *your* greatness before they can feel their own.

Let yourself RISE.

Be BOLD!

Be BIG!

Be CRAZY confident!

> Powerful people LOVE to SHINE.

Here is the journal entry I wrote the day after I began accepting my view of myself as a powerful leader. Warning: *I was a little excited.*

Saturday, September 19, 2015   4:30pm

I'm having this RUSH of inspiration about what my new sense of my POWER will mean for my career. How bold will I be? How radiant will I be? How confident will I be in promoting my products? I'm REALLY excited about this! The one bullet point in my list of Powerful People that is SHINING OUT to me, is the one about "not waiting for others to promote them."

Powerful people don't wait for others to promote them. They are so consumed with passion that they confidently radiate their joy in what they have created and effortlessly promote it with childlike glee.

I want to promote myself and my mission! I don't want to be ashamed anymore of shouting from the rooftops how passionate I am about the School for Dreamers! I am sensing that as I let go of my old paradigms, this new power and boldness is gonna attract people to us in large and full numbers! I have this sense that my POWER is about to be released in an exciting new way that's gonna totally skyrocket my mission!

Spirit, guide me. I'm READY to embrace, feel, know, and ACTIVATE my POWER.

I hereby LET GO of my old self. All sense of shame for shining, for boldness, for greatness, I hereby LET GO of all of this.

I am NEW.

I am CRAZY BOLD.

I am CRAZY CONFIDENT.

I promote my products with ecstatic, childlike boldness.

I let go of all insecure thoughts.

I KNOW the power in my book, my music album, and my School. It's TIME for unabashed BOLDNESS!!

Recruit! Say what you want!

Be specific about the kind of students you want!

I've ALWAYS KNOWN that if I TRULY believed in something, I'd be able to sell it.

It's TIME.

I'm ready to BE the most powerful, dynamic, inspirational version of me. Charismatic!

Charming! BOLD! Unashamed!

Effervescent!

Unapologetic!

I'm ready to activate my power.

What is POSSIBLE for me?

What is POSSIBLE for me as I fully clothe myself in this POWER?

What could happen?

What people could be attracted to us?

How many students could enroll?

How many lives could be changed?

By walking fully into my full energetic magnificence, what could happen?

I surrender ALL judgments about ASKING or PROMOTING.

I AM WORTHY of spreading the word about my products.

I AM WORTHY of talking boldly about the School.

I AM WORTHY of rallying SUPPORT in promoting my products.

I ADMIRE people who JOYFULLY promote their work because of their PASSION – you can FEEL the authenticity.

Be like a child!

*Like the author Jackie Lea Sommers – her ecstatic, childlike joy for her first novel, **Truest**, is contagious. I'm not turned off at all by the blog posts she writes as she boldly shares her enthusiasm about her book, day after day – I LOVE IT.*

It INSPIRES ME!!

THAT is how people will feel about me and my promoting.

When someone is authentically passionate about her work, you can FEEL it, and you are DRAWN to help her.

YES.

It's TIME. It's time to step up. It's time to passionately ASK for what I want.

> **Powerful people know what they want and they aren't afraid to ASK for it.**

What is POSSIBLE for me as I become BOLD about promoting myself and my mission?

ANYTHING and EVERYTHING is POSSIBLE!

Everything will grow.

I want to BE this person.

Spirit, guide me.

Show me how to be the most POWERFUL VERSION OF ME.

Let me fuel this passion into unashamed promotion of my products – the book, the album, and the School.

I embrace insane levels of passion and bold confidence to share my work with the world.

I KNOW the world needs it.

I'm READY to be the BOLDLY CONFIDENT NOELLE!!

Are you with me?

The Power of ASKING for What You Want

I used to think it was a sign of lack of trust in Spirit, to ASK others for help. But what I've realized now is that sometimes asking people for help is the best gift you can give them. As with everything, there's an appropriate powerful TIME to ask for support.

How do you know when it's time?

You know it's time to ask for help when you are guided by joyful energy to do so.

And as I've been practicing this, I've already started seeing powerful results.

Recently I realized that if I want to see powerful growth in the School for Dreamers -- if I want to see great testimonies from students on my website -- I need to ask for their help.

Does asking mean I'm needy?

Absolutely not.

Does it mean I'm not trusting Spirit?

Absolutely not.

But these are the thoughts I used to have that kept me from asking others for their help in supporting me and my mission.

Since I've begun asking for support -- emotional, financial, and promotional -- a big shift has occurred in our businesses.

We feel more connected to our audience, our finances are growing, and I'm receiving the blessing of testimonies from students in the School for Dreamers.

Here is one powerful review I received recently from one of my precious students, Carol. She just finished Course 1 (*Bliss Beyond Belief*) in the School and she has a dream of being a writer. I wrote an email to all the recent graduates of Course 1, asking if they would write a personal testimony for my website. Carol was the first to respond and I was catapulted into total BLISS as I read her beautiful words:

> *I recently turned 60. And I was at a crossroads trying to figure out what was going to be the next chapter in my journey. When I found Noelle, her YouTube channel and especially her book . . . I knew this was the road to go down because the title of the book had BLISS (something my brother taught me to live by) and the word DREAM in the course title of the School for Dreamers. I have always been a dreamer and I try and pay attention to my dreams. So I read the book and became a student.*
>
> *I am so glad I did! Noelle is an inspirational life coach. She was my cheerleader when I needed encouragement to go thru the weekly courses. It was often intense! It challenged me to be brave and follow*

my bliss! I was shown that I am a powerful, magical and creative spirit!

I encourage everyone who hears or reads this, to jump off the high dive into the pool of infinite possibilities.

Once you know WHO you truly are, you begin to live a powerful, magical, blissful life!

Thank you, Noelle, for being there for me.

I know that the writer in me is now, free!

I anxiously await the next course and book!

Carol Elek

To my beloved Carol: your dream has come true, my friend. You are definitely a writer – a beautiful writer! Thank you for contributing to my life through this powerful written testimony.

So you can see, that if I hadn't ASKED my students for their testimonies, *I* would not have been blessed by Carol's review, YOU would not have been blessed by it, and SHE would not have been blessed by writing it.

So stop thinking that it's weak or needy or untrusting to ask for support – whether emotional, financial, promotional, or otherwise.

We are meant to live in community.

We are designed to live in interdependence and to support each other.

And how will I know how I can support *you*, if you don't tell me?

You have a tribe of people who are *waiting* to support you, who will be BLESSED, who will find THEIR purpose by supporting you. But they won't know what role they can fill in your life if you don't tell them what you need.

This is what it means to become BOLD about your life and your mission, my friend. It means letting go of those old paradigms that just aren't serving you anymore. It means opening yourself up to criticism. Because when you start asking for support -- especially financial support -- people will judge you.

As a leader, you're just going to have to accept that when you build a brand, a mission, something worth living for –

some people are going to LOVE it and some people are going to HATE it.

When people start judging what you're doing, you can celebrate! Because it means you are being bold and specific and taking a stand for something meaningful. People usually don't take time to criticize something that's lukewarm. They criticize when something is bold and it strikes a chord with them – it AFFECTS them. And that's a good thing! It means you're on the right track. It means you have FIRE and PASSION and that people SEE and CARE about what you're doing.

Focus on those who LOVE what you're doing. Focus on your tribe. Focus on those who are finding their PURPOSE in life through joining your mission.

Because I can tell you, that when I read a review like the one by Carol, saying that because of the School for Dreamers she now knows WHO she is and the *writer in her is now free* –

well all of the judgmental criticism I've ever received for being vulnerably bold with my mission

just *disappears,*

like a faint mist that's obliterated

by the strong winds of heavenly support and love.

It's a hurricane of support and connectedness!

Ego is completely forgotten when LOVE floods your life.

Be COURAGEOUS!

Be BOLD!

ASK for what you want!

Full support for your mission will overwhelm you with joy as you step into your power!

Chapter 6

The Power of UNIQUENESS

Launch Your Dream Business, Your Way

You may have been drawn to this book from the title and thought that by reading it you would learn the necessary steps you can take to be able to quit your day job and start your dream business.

Maybe you thought I would give you the 10 steps for launching your own business -- that you could learn them, start implementing them and be on your way to success and freedom. And I'm sure there are lots of books out there that will give you those steps.

But this is definitely not one of them.

My intention for this book is to give you something much *much* greater than a guidebook or a blueprint.

I want to give you something much more lasting than 10 steps.

I want to give you a *secret* I've discovered.

This piece of treasured knowledge is so rich, so valuable, so simple yet so life-changing --

that if you are READY to receive it,

to enjoy it,

to explore it,

to fully utilize it,

you will not only be able to launch your dream business,

you will not *only* be able to live the life of your deepest dreams,

you will literally be able to *change* the world.

There have been many truths that have set me free throughout these past 7 years since my big spiritual awakening in 2008. But the truth I give you in this chapter has been one of the most profound and life-changing for me.

Perhaps this truth (which I will give you soon) is so life-changing because I grew up in the Evangelical Christian church, and I was taught that I couldn't trust my desires. I was taught that my desires were inherently sinful, because *I* was inherently sinful. I was taught that because I couldn't trust my own desires, I needed guidance from a mentor, from a spiritual mother or father. I was taught I couldn't trust ME.

And even in the self-help, New Age, New Thought world to which I gravitated upon leaving religion, I was still told I needed a mentor, or I wouldn't be able to succeed.

There is nothing wrong with having a mentor, and I make a living being a mentor to people, so I'm not saying that it is a negative thing to have a mentor, by any means. But every time I heard this advice, I cringed. It just confirmed for me that I couldn't trust myself. That I needed outside guidance. That I wasn't enough, that I couldn't be the leader of my life. That I couldn't hear directly from Spirit and trust myself.

And this idea, that I couldn't fully trust my own voice, that I needed outside guidance, that I needed to follow what others were doing, that I needed accountability, always made me very depressed.

This belief was so ingrained into my psyche, it has taken years to fully remove it. And there are still times -- like just last night when I received an email from a fan in which he gave me advice for my spiritual life, pointing out an area in which he thought I was blind -- there are times when I am still tempted to doubt myself. There are still times like this when I fall into the old trap of not trusting my gut, and I lose all my power, in an instant.

So after years of soul-searching and practicing and listening to my own voice, I have discovered this truth, which I now give to you, in the hopes that you will be able to fully receive it, fully enjoy it, and embrace it *so completely* that it will change your life, as it has mine.

So here it is:

You are more powerful than you have yet fathomed. You have everything inside you. You have *direct access* to all the knowledge and wisdom the Universe has to offer. You don't need ANYTHING outside of yourself on this earth to guide you. You don't need a mentor, or a spiritual parent. You don't need an earthly teacher. You are completely plugged in to Source, to God -- you have never been separate from God, never have been and never will be -- and the only thing keeping you from fully and clearly hearing what to DO next, is your inability to trust yourself and the wisdom within you. YOU have everything you need for your business and your mission.

Now, being that I make my living being a spiritual teacher, you would think I would not want to tell you this, right?

I'm working myself out of a job here – LOL!

And yet we are all on different parts of this journey. The journey of being able to trust ourselves takes some time.

And on that journey, it can be very helpful to have a guide.

But as a teacher, the most important lesson I will ever teach you, is that YOU can be your own teacher.

That YOU have access DIRECTLY to all the guidance you will ever need.

You have a unique role on this earth. You know it, you feel it.

You've always longed to fulfill your destiny.

And I'm here to tell you, from deep and intentional personal experience, that you already know, deep within you, what to do next.

I can't give you the 10 steps for how to launch your own business, because you are the keeper of those unique steps for YOU. Those steps are lying dormant inside you, waiting to be awakened. They are unique. Your path is YOURS. It is adventurous, it is crazy, it is unique, it is different, it is what happens when you decide to be FULLY YOU and trust yourself.

Everything I've accomplished in my businesses these past few years has happened as a direct result of trusting myself, of allowing myself to be *inspired* by what other leaders and entrepreneurs are doing, but not thinking that I need to do it exactly how they've done it or copy them at all.

> Powerful people don't copy what other leaders are doing. They listen to their OWN VOICE and do it their own way.

People love to attach themselves to a WAY.

And they make these *strong* statements about this, because it worked that way for *them*.

134

Statements like,

"You HAVE to have a newsletter."

"You can't blog every day -- that's crazy, that's not even good marketing -- that will never work."

"You have to spend *most* of your time on marketing and promoting your work."

"You have to have a mentor."

"You HAVE to read this book."

"You HAVE to spend a lot of time editing your book before you publish it."

"You have to grow your audience before you can do a successful launch of anything."

All of these are real pieces of advice that at one time I chose to ignore.

I decided to TRUST my own voice.

> Powerful people don't need advice or approval from others. They are so in tune with their own voice, they get everything they need here: encouragement, guidance, and energy.

Sometimes the advice is really good and I end up doing it later, like the newsletter thing – but at the time someone told me that, I wasn't *ready* to do a newsletter. And the thought that I NEEDED to do one in order to build my business, depressed me, because I wasn't ready to do one.

So here's the key:

Start trusting that your own voice -- your Highest Self, Spirit, God (however you choose to connect with that still small voice inside) -- will GUIDE you for EVERY next step you need to take.

Don't listen to all the well-meaning voices out there that tell you HOW you need to build your business or your dream life.

YOU are the ONLY ONE who really knows the best way for you.

And if you're an entrepreneur, you're gonna be doing something new and exciting and different.

If you're a trail-blazer, how can you possible think that following what other people are doing is going to make you successful?

How will you blaze a trail if it's already blazed?

And I think you are meant to be a leader.

You are meant to blaze a new trail, create a new way, do something different.

And the only way to know which way to go, is to start listening within. Surrender to Spirit. Seek within. That's where all the answers are for YOU.

The further along I travel on this journey of being a leader and a business owner, the more I have decided to have strong blinders up to what other leaders are doing.

Sometimes I'm inspired by something a leader does, but for the most part, I just need to ignore what other leaders are doing, because it distracts me from my own mission.

I know that if there's something I need to know, Spirit will ALWAYS bring it to my attention. I don't ever worry anymore that I'm missing out on a truth or a certain way to do something, because I've learned that the unique path for me is always given to me, as I look within.

And when there's something for me to see or learn, I always see it and learn it in the right time.

There's a LOT of information floating around out there, my friend. How do you know what to listen to?

I encourage you to start first, by TRUSTING that you will be guided to the right information, as you need it.

And as you seek within FIRST -- get to know yourself, learn to listen to your own voice, learn to TRUST your own voice -- you will know when outside information is to be utilized, by THIS barometer:

If outside information or advice gives you JOY and ENERGY and makes you feel inspired and it resonates with you, then it's for YOU!

If outside information or advice makes you feel HEAVY, DEPRESSED, STRESSED, BEHIND, ANXIOUS, or just plain WEIGHED DOWN– it's NOT FOR YOU. Simply hit the delete button. Say "thanks but no thanks."

Keep in mind, that it might be really good advice, but it's just not the right time. But if it's not the right TIME for that advice, that there's no reason whatsoever to think about it right now.

Let me give you an example from my own experience.

MARKETING has always been one of those heavy topics for me.

Whenever I used to hear anyone talking about advice for marketing or promoting, I would get sick to my stomach.

Because I just had no energy for it.

I didn't enjoy thinking about it.

I wanted to DREAM and CREATE.

I knew I wanted a BIG audience, but whenever I saw what others were doing to *get* a big audience, I got depressed. I read the advice, I watched the videos on YouTube about how to gain more subscribers, and I felt ill.

I just didn't have energy for it.

And the reason I felt ILL, is because I WANTED a big audience, but I didn't want to DO what they were saying I needed to do to get one. So I was AFRAID that if I didn't do what they said, I would fail.

Finally I just began to trust and accept that I could do it my own way in my own time. That I could trust my energy for everything that needed to be done.

I began to trust that LIFE was guiding me to the unique path for me, and that even though the "experts" were saying there was a certain way to build an audience, I didn't need to listen to the outside experts, because the only EXPERT in MY life, for MY path, is ME -- the ME that's connected to Spirit, to God.

My Highest Self knows the way.

And I can trust that.

And so I started putting up blinders to all the expert, well-meaning advice. And believe me, when you are running towards your destiny and you begin sharing yourself with the world, you will start to receive advice from every angle. Because people want to help you.

This is SO critical, my friend. If you want to run your own race, blaze your own trail, be true to who you are, and ENJOY every moment doing it, then you must simply IGNORE all the advice that doesn't lift you up.

Don't worry about it – just ignore it!

Trust that God will guide you to the right information when you need it.

You can't do everything at once.

Stop comparing yourself to others.

There was a time when I consumed every self-help book and YouTube video I could, because I was growing and learning and finding myself.

But now?

I hardly ever read anything or watch any videos whatsoever.

I'm in creating mode.

I'm tapped into my own creative flow, and so I protect that space.

I can't birth great spiritual treasure into the world if I'm distracted by what other teachers or authors are doing.

I focus on what I'm doing.

And I find true bliss here!

There is so much treasure inside me, I don't have time to look outside myself.

I have an important mission to release this treasure into the world, and that's where all my energy is focused.

And I've seen, time and time again, that a piece of advice I once chose to ignore, has *later* emerged as something I organically felt the desire to do, such as start an email list (newsletter).

I can't tell you how much I agonized a few years ago about not having an email list.

I knew it was important but I just didn't have the joyful energy to work on it.

And in the most magical time in the most perfect easy way, when the right time came to start an email list -- OMG was it effortless and fun!

No stress, no striving, no pressure.

And now my email list is growing and I absolutely LOVE my newsletter – *The Awaken Weekly*. It's one of my favorite times of the week, creating that newsletter. And every Friday, hundreds of people are blessed by it. Because it's the right time for it in my life and my business.

The more I trust, the more I experience magic. The more I let go of striving and pushing, the more everything just effortlessly flows. Work is Play and Play is Work – there is no difference when you're in the flow. Right now it's a Sunday morning, I'm sitting at Starbucks writing this book for you, and I'm in total bliss. Is this work? Yes, but it's also play. It's total bliss.

It's time to release that kind of bliss into YOUR life. You've tried it the other way – we all have.

Another piece of advice you will hear is that you have to work REALLY HARD to make a living at your own business.

I don't work *hard* at all.

I can't even believe how easy my life is.

Every day feels like vacation.

My work -- leading the School for Dreamers, writing books like this, writing *The Awaken Weekly*, producing my YouTube show, writing music, speaking/singing to live audiences, writing in my journal -- it's all the same. Pure play. Pure joy.

And now we're making *money* doing what we love. Vince and I get to travel the world, living our passion, doing an important purpose, while having most of our time free to just be together. We go on long walks by the beach, watch movies in our cozy van, hang out at Starbucks, go out to eat, and of course, cuddle.

It doesn't get much better than this.

Sometimes we just look at each other and say,

"Is this REAL? Is this really our life? Did we really just take off in our car 8 months ago?"

It feels like a lifetime ago.

Our life feels like one long vacation, except much better, because we're doing something purposeful.

We're changing the world.

We're showing people, just by the life that we live, that they can let go of society's idea of what success is, and be truly successful TODAY.

You can let go of all those obligations you think are so permanent, and start trusting in the Universe to provide for your mission, as you fearlessly walk into the life you were BORN to live on this earth.

As you let go of your fears, as you let go of what others think of you, as you let go of all the reasons why you CAN'T live your dream life *now*, and start to RUN towards the life you've always imagined, you will be surprised at how everything starts working out.

Resources, people, opportunities -- it will all flow to you as you follow your bliss.

Don't spend your life working at a job you don't love just because the world tells you that's what NORMAL people do.

Do you really want to be *normal*?

I don't.

I want to be different. I want to be extraordinary.

I want to be ME.

The joy of allowing yourself to be fully YOU, will overwhelm you if you let it. Once you make the decision to be absolutely TRUE to your deepest desires, no matter what anyone else thinks, you will witness miracles.

You will feel your power growing.

Every single choice you make in support of who YOU are, is a powerful step towards your destiny.

Start today by simply asking yourself,

Where is my heart right now?

If I only had one YEAR left to live on this earth, what would I really want to do with my time?

If I only had one MONTH left to live, what concerns or worries would just float away?

If I only had one WEEK left to live, how BOLD would I be?

How FEARLESS would I be?

My friend, you may know how much money you have in the bank, but I guarantee that you don't know how much TIME you have left on this earth. You don't know how much time you have left to be this unique version of you. This is your most precious resource. How are you going to spend it?

The way may seem cloudy. You may not even be able to feel what it would be like to have all your time free to do what you want. Maybe you don't even KNOW what you really want.

So let my life be a beacon of hope for you, because you and I are connected. I used to be where you are. I had all the same doubts and fears and limiting thoughts. I had all the same insecurities. I had all the same obligations and financial stressors.

And yet, here I am – FREE.

Free to live my purpose, to live a life that's BETTER than I ever dreamed.

Free to be the CEO of a growing mission-driven business.

Free to ENJOY every moment of my life.

Free to change the world.

Free to inspire YOU.

So take it from me: You can live this life too.

NOT by following the specific steps I've taken, but by looking within. You have all the answers inside you.

Start by envisioning the HIGHEST version of you that you can possible imagine, and meet with that person for coffee every day. Talk to that person, get to know that person, *become* that person.

Because that person IS you.

You are more powerful, more brilliant, more spectacular, more MAGNIFICENT and more NEEDED than you have ever dared dream.

So start dreaming. Start getting to know yourself. Start trusting yourself.

There is a world out here waiting for all the unique treasures YOU were meant to give. If you don't share your gifts, no one ever will. They are UNIQUE to you.

Don't die with your song still within you. The music of you is waiting to be released. When it's released, it will bring hope, healing, inspiration, encouragement, and awakening to everyone who needs it.

You will change the world, just by being fully and fearlessly YOU.

YOU are enough.

YOU are needed.

YOU are powerful.

Activate your power today, by allowing yourself to feel the ECSTASY of who you really are!

Addendum

Powerful People Quotes

The Power of VISION

Powerful people aren't afraid to FEEL. They know that great power comes from embracing EVERY human emotion: anger, pain, fear, passion, joy, and love.

Powerful people pay no attention to current circumstances that don't line up with their vision. Their eyes are set like laser beams on their dream life and purpose.

Powerful people know when to REST and when to ACT. They don't strive or push. They know that all action is easy and effortless as they rest in WHO THEY ARE.

The Power WITHIN

Powerful people know that their greatest treasure is found WITHIN.

Powerful people are insanely HAPPY regardless of external circumstances.

Powerful people know how to hear their own voice clearly. They trust their desires no matter what anyone else thinks.

Powerful people don't look for blame in any situation. They give thanks for EVERYTHING and only ask "What can I learn from this?"

Powerful people know that their greatest power is in surrendering to Spirit.

Powerful people value true knowledge gained from personal experience, rather than information or formal education.

Powerful people fully embrace their Divinity AND their humanity.

Powerful people know that everything they need is within them.

Powerful people live fully in the NOW, knowing the present moment is all there is, and that it is MAGICAL, LIMITLESS and POWERFUL.

The Power of FOCUS

Saying No

Powerful people joyfully say NO to everything they don't want to do. They live from passion, not obligation.

Criticism and Praise

Powerful people are unattached to both criticism and praise. Their energy comes from within, not from anything external.

Create a SPACE to Be You

Powerful people fiercely guard their time, money, and energy. They know that they will be guided in JOY when it is the right time to GIVE their resources.

Relationships

Powerful people have powerful boundaries. They let others live their own lives.

Powerful people fiercely guard their heart. They only allow people who UPLIFT them into their inner circle, regardless of the past, or family ties.

Powerful people let go of their family of origin, knowing that every person on earth is their brother and sister.

The Power of ABUNDANCE

Powerful people TRUST the Universe to provide for everything in their lives.

Powerful people have extravagant love for themselves and this naturally spills over to bless everyone who encounters them.

Powerful people know that Life is abundant, and so they FREELY receive and FREELY give, guided by JOY, not obligation.

Powerful people fully ENJOY their lives. Their work is play and their play is work – there is no difference.

Powerful people easily attract every resource needed for their mission by simply BEING themselves.

Powerful people know their power. They take responsibility for life, knowing they are co-creators with God.

Powerful people don't wait for HOW their dream will come true. They focus on the vision and start running towards it, knowing they are supported by Life.

The Power of BOLDNESS

Powerful people don't apologize for what they need, what they want, or who they are.

Powerful people know what they want and they aren't afraid to ASK for it.

Powerful people don't wait for their hero to launch them. They know that THEY are the HERO in their story.

Powerful people LOVE to SHINE.

Powerful people don't wait to react to life's events. They create their own life events and run joyfully on their own path.

Powerful people know how to embrace their fear, not fight it. They transform anxiety into passionate energy.

Powerful people KNOW WHO THEY ARE. They aren't ashamed to feel and know their MAGNIFICENCE.

Powerful people don't wait for others to promote them. They are so consumed with passion that they confidently radiate their joy in what they have created and effortlessly promote it with childlike glee.

Powerful people know that the world needs what they have to give.

The Power of UNIQUENESS

Powerful people don't try to fit in. They choose a unique path, and others follow them.

Powerful people don't copy what other leaders are doing. They listen to their OWN VOICE, and do it their own way.

Powerful people don't need advice or approval from others. They are so in tune with their own voice, they get everything they need here: encouragement, guidance, and energy.

Powerful people know that RULES and LIMITS don't apply to them.

About the Author

Noelle Marie Amendola is a dynamic spiritual leader, motivational speaker, singer/songwriter, author, and founder of the School for Dreamers.

Her life mission is to AWAKEN the world to the truth that every person is magnificent and has a powerful, unique purpose.

She and her husband Vince live full-time on the road in order to spread her message of LOVE and JOY.

You can connect with Noelle at

www.noellemarie.com

Made in the USA
Charleston, SC
03 August 2016